Wally and Zizza's Amazing Journey

WALLY AND ZIZZA'S AMAZING JOURNEY

A VANRENEN SAGA

LOUIS VANRENEN

Matador
9 Priory Business Park,
Wistow Road, Kibworth Beauchamp,
Leicestershire. LE8 0RX
Tel: 0116 279 2299
Email: books@troubador.co.uk
Web: www.troubador.co.uk/matador
Twitter: @matadorbooks

ISBN 978 1789014 716

British Library Cataloguing in Publication Data.
A catalogue record for this book is available from the British Library.

Printed and bound in Great Britain by 4edge Limited
Typeset in 12pt Minion Pro by Troubador Publishing Ltd, Leicester, UK

Matador is an imprint of Troubador Publishing Ltd

This book is dedicated to Wally and Zizza

CONTENTS

Introduction		ix
1.	Setting the scene	1
2.	England, where it started	13
3.	India, how did that happen?	31
4.	How did the British end up in India?	36
5.	Akbar and the Moghuls and European expansion	43
6.	Go east	51
7.	Wally and Zizza, the newlyweds arrive in India	57
8.	Life in India for the British	62
9.	The Northwest Frontier and its importance for the family	73
10.	Colonel Holdich and the Northwest Frontier	86
11.	Notable people on the Northwest Frontier	95
12.	Wally's world	108
13.	People and places of India during the Raj	133
14.	Gulmarg: The mountain resort	152
15.	Renala; Ysobel and Louis	162
16.	Hazel and the end of Renala	189
17.	Darshan	204
18.	The amazing journey continues	211
Epilogue		230

INTRODUCTION

THE FAMILY

Human beings share many experiences in life but, perhaps, none as dramatic as the day of birth. We all emerge from the womb of our mother, an incredible fact. A baby, a tiny person, enters the world, the beginning of a great adventure. Each stage can be explained, but each is a miracle: the fertilization, the development in the womb, and the creation in a few months of a miniature human being perfectly formed. Everyone, including the most celebrated—Einstein, Shakespeare, and Augustus Caesar—were tiny, helpless infants. In those early months all are nurtured by a mother or a surrogate. And all become part of a family with a mother and father. This nucleus — with some permutations — is a foundation of our lives. There are some, of course, who are orphans or have one parent, but these often and thankfully find a nourishing support group.

Each family is different, with varying degrees of stability, happiness, and friendship, and whether we like it or not, we are a part of this connection for life. Some families are happy, some challenged, but most experience a mixture including friendship, disagreement, joy, and discovery. Whatever the nature of this family, the experience is always an adventure where we first learn how to live in the world. It is not always easy, sometimes very difficult, but it is a remarkable kaleidoscope of experiences—mundane, challenging, and exciting. Our parents are the first people that we know, especially in the early years. For good and bad, they loom larger than life and leave an indelible impression on us, something some of us in adulthood try to deny. They, hopefully, leave us with hopes and values that run deep and assist us in the challenge of living.

When we become independent adults, the family is still part of us, even for those who rebel. There are some who drift away, others who stay close, but the fact remains: We are a part of a chain that goes back generations, one wave after another. And, no matter how much some may wriggle or run, they cannot escape the family and its heritage: it is imbedded in our genes, subconscious, and life. And often the influences and results are very good. Each family emerges from a specific place and history, within an atmosphere and culture, and each has a story that is diverse, interesting, even remarkable.

This book tells the story of my parents, Wally and Zizza. Their journey was truly amazing. They lived on four continents, including India and Africa, during most of the tumultuous twentieth century. During this remarkable span they would raise a family, and finally settle in America during the exciting decade of the 1960s. Both would engage in a healthy examination of their identity and life purpose. As in all families, there were times of struggle, loss, adventure, and happiness. And like all parents they had their flaws and strengths, but they, I can honestly say, tried their best in often trying circumstances.

There is no "school" for parenting. We learn from parents and relatives, and sometimes these models are not so good. The teenagers assume they know best and easily find fault, but one day they too will be parents. It is true, however, that parents come in different colors: some are born to parent, some are at a loss, others learn slowly. Many stumble and fall, then get up again; they try hard and become quite adept. But good parenting is founded on being an alert and responsible human being, and, in the end, it is the art of living well that we must all strive for.

We all share another fascinating fact: We come from a chain of family going back generations, back to the beginning of the human experiment on this planet. Though most of us know little about our distant relatives, we might have had the pleasure of knowing our grandparents. But we all go back into a forgotten and mysterious past. We also move forward. The chain can live on with youngsters who will in time marry and have children. Whether or not we have children, we are still a part of the human family that, as the Bible and science tells us, has a common origin.

ONE

SETTING THE SCENE

I had thought about this project, this book, for many years but never thought I would actually complete it. This is the story of my parents, Wally and Zizza, and the great adventure of their lives, which, in a sense, is ongoing even though they have passed on. For this project, I had a very good motivation: a respect and love for them and their lives—not only for them but their parents and relatives, and the generation that followed them, including my two sisters, my brother, and their children.

Wally and Zizza's journey was truly remarkable: It spanned much of the twentieth century in four continents: Europe, Asia, Africa, and America, a decade or more in each. They were born into the British Empire just before the terrible conflagration of World War I and in the days when the empire began to crack. They were both British but came from completely different backgrounds and families. They would spend their last decades in America, itself once a British colony, and happily integrate themselves into American life. And that was very good.

As a little girl, Zizza could not pronounce Elizabeth, resulting in a marvelous nickname that followed her through life. She was born into a simple, quiet English village, her father the local vicar. The region, Kent, still retained qualities of the Victorian era. Wally, part of a roaming colonial family, was born in what is now Pakistan, and lived most of his life far from home, the England of his family. They were both born into a great empire, but Wally's family was an active part of that empire for two centuries, connected to the army stationed in many corners of the globe.

Yet Zizza and Wally shared something in common with all people. They lived through so much, as do all parents, saw so much change, and encountered many kinds of people. They experienced births, deaths, tragedies, triumphs, joys, laughter, tears, losses, and radical changes on our planet. They spent good times in England, India, Africa—a palette as different as you can imagine. In a quiet triumph, they would live their last years on the border of the Rocky Mountains, Americans, in fact, in their last decades.

The bulk of this project involves their early lives in England, their marriage, and the move to India, as newlyweds, just prior to World War II, and their departure by boat from India—on their way to England and South Africa. If I have time and inclination, Book II will be their life in Africa and America.

Almost everyone has mixed feelings about their parents while we live with them. We do not fully appreciate what they have done to make our lives better; we find fault with them (and they are far from perfect); and often, we take them for granted. My father, Wally, was not easy to live with. He was quiet, moody, and short-tempered. He drank too much, and he had some deep regrets. He had suffered terribly during World War II and came back wounded physically and emotionally, although he never spoke about it, never talked about being a soldier. He no doubt suffered from what we now call post-traumatic stress disorder. And why not? Those of us who have never been to war do not realize how horrible it is, 24 hours a day, 7 days a week, to be subject to sleeplessness, terrible and senseless violence, noise, grief, fear, anger, and terror. He fought in two horrible regions: the jungle war in Burma—where the British stemmed the Japanese invasion of India—and the desert war in North Africa, fighting

Rommel and his Nazi army. But he retained a quiet dignity in his last years, turning to a deep spiritual search which had an affirmative influence on me and others.

In Boulder, Colorado, where he spent his last years, he enjoyed gardening and taking care of his business matters. He had a circle of friends and activities, and most people considered him eccentric, with his muffled British accent and his unique mannerisms. He was, after all, an old British Indian cavalry man. Sometimes a tender side would emerge; for example, his love for our dogs (he was the only person in town who took the golden retriever into the bank—no one would dare protest). Never a warm and cozy father, we shared through the garden, dogs, and our tea time with Zizza.

My mother, an easy-going person, had many good qualities, but she suffered—as everyone does—in her life, which was not all easy or fun. She out-lived her two daughters. But she enjoyed people and life, always trying different activities, never stagnating. She loved flowers, painting, and friends. She was especially kind as a mother and grandmother. After my sister Val died prematurely, she cared for her children, Roderick and Vivienne, for many years.

It has been almost a decade since she has left, and 36 years since my father died at Memorial Hospital in Boulder, Colorado. I have had time to reflect about them and appreciate them even more, grateful to them for my life and all the good things they did to make my life better. Gratitude is a wonderful emotion to truly feel each day—a gratefulness for this precious life. Without my parents, I would not be able to feel the depths of this quality emotion.

I had the means to tell their remarkable story: I am a writer, a lover of history and family, and I possess some unusual papers and photographs from their lives. I inherited this family treasure chest, tucked away in a wooden box, carted around for several decades to various basements and attics. Occasionally, I would open the box and admire some images or papers, but, like almost everyone, I would have left these hidden away, to be discovered by my son or daughter after my passing. "Oh, look, Gabe," my daughter might have said one day, "Dad has a pile of photographs and papers from his past." And Gabe would have drily responded, "Oh, that's pretty cool." And in their later lives the box would, if it were lucky, travel from one storage space to another. But, thanks to several influences, something very different has occurred. I have created a book from the contents of the box, and, more important, from their lives.

About some of the family history, I am limited, and I make no claims to be a general historian. I apologize for any errors or omissions in the family history, but I tried my best with the information I had. For example, there is much about my father's family that I can never know, and no one is living whom I can ask. And during his life he was not the kind of father who would regale me with stories about his family. On that front he was quiet. But I do have some advantages. I lived near my parents for a quarter of a century, I heard stories, met relatives, and absorbed some of their past.

I was born in Africa, after the Indian chapter, and in my youth lived in the shadow of their lives in India: hearing of Renala, the grand old family estate, the language—they both used Hindu words—and my father spoke the English of British India (more on that later). I heard stories and names, saw pictures, and read books about India. Years later, in my late twenties, I toured India for five glorious months. This fabulous journey, by the way, was my honeymoon with Johnna. With her, I had my own amazing Indian experience.

But there is more: I inherited my father's photograph albums and some papers; my mother's album (going back to childhood in England in the 1920s); and my grandmother Ysobel's remarkable photographs (and a few papers). Ysobel, my father's mother, spent much of her life in British India. I never met Ysobel, as she died three years before I was born, but I feel close to her. As we will see, she had a storied life and was a wonderful human being.

I also inherited my great Uncle Louis' album with some of his papers. This treasure trove came via a long and circuitous route: Because Louis had no children, my father inherited his papers and photographs, which arrived in America from India via South Africa, where he is buried. Uncle Louis—my namesake—operated an indigo estate in what is now Pakistan. Indigo, much valued, was used for a dye. Some of his photographs are fascinating: historical, personal, and artistic. Some, like my grandmother's, are quite lovely. Neither were professional photographers, but they captured some wonderful images from their exotic homes and travels. A few of the photographs are over one hundred years old, including a handful of "studio" shots. Some are remarkable for their artistry, but I will never know the facts—equipment, professional help, and, in some cases, who was behind this artistry. Nevertheless, the photographs are here for us to see and admire.

In short, I had a precious cache of gems that I wanted to share with family, friends, and others. As the project developed—and it was thrilling—I knew I was compiling a unique book. Not many people have the resources and tools to illustrate a family history. But this is more than my family history; it is also the poignant journey of all of us, of all of humanity. We all are born into a time and place, which might be different from another, but at the root we share similar dreams, desires, and needs. We all share common experiences: the challenges and joys of adolescence, the adventure of schooling, the relationship with parents, the coming of maturity and getting married, the adventure or pain of moving to a new place, the various recreations we all enjoy, the fact of aging, and even more, the mysterious fact of dying. We are all born onto this beautiful planet to enjoy it for a short time and hopefully come to some understanding of why we are here.

We are all born into a particular place and time, but there are key experiences that we share. Everyone, for example, has their geographic place they love: a cottage on the border of a lake, a townhouse in the city, a mountain trail, or a farm on a prairie. We all share the common sorrows, losses, and tragedies; we all share the joys and pains of relationships and times of happiness. We are all born into a miraculous body that has many gifts, but most important, the ability to carry us through a lifetime of simple pleasures. We all share a sense of transience: We are here for a short time. And during our moment here, we sense that we must take advantage of our time and develop tools and strategies for quality living.

There is much to consider in all this. My parents and all their friends have gone forever. But I do not think that the purpose of this project—or of life—is to become trapped in nostalgia, regret, or fear. I see that for me and those whom I have respected, there is a process in the act of the living where we become closer to the pulse of life–that pulse is not personal, it is not me or you. It is something we all share. That pulse is closely allied with what great sages call our essence or true self–that core that lies beneath the chatter and business of the surface personality. I believe it is one of the great tragedies of life to just believe in this external person—the me, me, me—who is infatuated with his or her story. We are greater than we realize—or were taught in schools—but not in a small, egoistic sense.

I am so grateful to have come to this profound and satisfying realization. I could not have done it without my parents. In their own way, they were on this search, following in the footsteps of some of their ancestors. I now realize why I feel a love for Ysobel, Wally's mother, even though I never met her. While she might never have articulated these hopes, she was on a journey of discovery, and the same was true for Zizza.

In their later years, both Wally and Zizza would embark on a search for a deeper identity, studying with several authentic teachers. My father met respected philosopher John Bennet in England, and Bennet had studied with the master G.I. Gurdjieff, who taught, among other things, a way of living in the present. Today, topics like mindfulness, living in the present, and meditation are everywhere: scientific journals, books, and television. Wally and Zizza began this exploration before these topics became popular.

Wally and Zizza shared an unconventional search for meaning in life, for a deeper identity and a more inclusive perspective. The deeper essence that we all share is not bound to small self, family, or nation: It goes beyond these false boundaries toward a transcendental freedom. It is strange to say that these two ex-British colonials, who had come out of the Edwardian era, would become authentic seekers, exploring topics that today are popular, such as integrity of the body, mind, and feeling. But we have seen this hunger emerge in people from all cultures, societies, and time.

There were intrepid seekers in Rome, Greece, Palestine, India, Africa, and Japan. Some have names like Buddha, Jesus, Marcus Aurelius (the Roman emperor), Socrates; some are Christian hermits, Zen masters from Japan, Sufis from Islam, and many others—always an undercurrent in the "normal" interests of their place and time. And today, despite all the political or religious nonsense, we have our wise people, men and women, from all nations and cultures. One meaning of the word "wise" is "to see clearly." We cannot see clearly from the heart and mind if we are all cluttered and noisy inside. Contemplation and silence play a major role in the quality of life.

All the great teachers include moments of quiet in their lives. I, for example, have admired Nelson Mandela, Mahatma Gandhi, G.I. Gurdjieff, Henry David Thoreau, Anthony Bloom (a Russian Orthodox priest), and several women who live a life of wisdom. Wisdom can inhabit anyone—from any culture, sex, or religion—who seeks a quality life during their sojourn on earth.

Zizza's father, Alan Bruce Ronald, a modest village vicar, also shared a hunger that went beyond the conventional strivings. A scholarly minister who had studied Ralph Waldo Emerson and St. Paul at Cambridge, he maintained an active search through his adult life. His father and brothers were enterprising businessmen engaged in the Australian wool trade, while Alan Bruce took a different path in life. My mother followed in his footsteps, and my father, I only recently realized, followed in the steps of his mother.

Like most, I have a deep interest in the mystery of life, birth, and death, and the adventure that we all embark on at a very early age. Lives come and go, as do the generations and centuries. Empires, like people, have a life span: an exuberant youth, a comfortable and sometimes luxurious middle age with some problems, and a slow (or sometimes sudden) decline.

I was born in a remote British colony in Africa in the twilight of the once-great British Empire. I remember that when I was a boy I would pore over my father's 1930 historical map of the world. On that map, one quarter of the planet was pink—the color that designated British colonies. That included the giant country of India, over one third of Africa, and many holdings elsewhere in the Pacific, the Far East (such as Hong Kong), and the Caribbean. We may forget that Australia, a huge country, was not too long ago a British colony, as was Canada and America, the country I inhabit now. Amazing that a tiny island with a tiny population would for more than 400 years dominate the planet. Britannia ruled the oceans; its mighty navies controlled the sea routes. But it was also a leader in literature, science, and industry. Britain produced some of the giants of world literature: Shakespeare, Dickens, and many others. Many pioneering scientists were British, including Darwin, Faraday, and Maxwell—the last two were giants in electricity. Dr. Alexander Fleming, who discovered penicillin (the first great antibiotic), was British. Countless poets, writers, artists, and musicians, many of world stature, emerged from this dynamic but tiny nation over four centuries.

Great Britain in the nineteenth century was a mighty industrial power. Its northern cities teemed with coal, chimneys, trains, and bustling factories. It was one of the first industrial giants, churning out machines, trains, tools, farm equipment, and much else, exporting all over the planet. It has long been surpassed by America and more recently Japan and China. But during the nineteenth century, Great Britain traded all over the planet: spices, fabrics, and minerals from India; foods, people, raw material, and much else poured into the port cities of England.

In my early years I lived in the faded glory of this great empire as it began to be dismantled by freedom movements around the planet, quite appropriately: the colonies deserved self-rule. By the time I was a teenager (an American one!), the empire had virtually disappeared, holding out in a few isolated islands and cities. Hong Kong, once a thriving British colony, became incorporated into China.

I grew up as a little empire boy, filled with the propaganda and romance of the great British Empire. I read the rousing books and comics about heroic empire soldiers; the explorers who first explored the planet. I idolized Captain Cook, who opened up the Pacific Ocean; I marveled at the exploits of the British explorers of Africa, including Captain Richard Burton, swordsman, multi-linguist, scholar, and explorer. One of his many adventures was the ill-fated expedition to seek the source of the Nile, a tale that fascinated the world. I read about Clive of India, who started as a private in the British India Company army and ended as a vainglorious and wealthy general, almost legendary in the battles he won in India. He helped open India to British control, but Clive retired to Britain bulging with gout, money, and corruption. The British, with ingenuity, hard work, and guns, would forge a mighty empire in giant India, but their prime strength, as in all empires, was abundant self-confidence. But that too is mortal. Remember America in the 1950s, or Rome in the time of Augustus Caesar.

Winston Churchill, the great British leader, once famously said that India would always be under English power. He was a remarkable man, also a dreamer. India was an ancient land, filled with centuries of experience and wisdom, with tidal waves of high culture; if the British introduced them, for good and bad, to the modern world, the Indians could well take care of themselves.

By 1860, the great patchwork of British Indian lands coalesced, almost magically—and often brutally—into a huge empire: the great jewel in the crown. The Raj, an Indian word meaning rule, strutted around for almost one hundred years. The British—and by this term I mean British people who lived in India—ruling class, as ostentatious as any ruling class in history, displayed magnificent palaces, marches, and sporting extravaganzas. A strange fact about British India is that they built some of the grandest railway terminals in history, Anglo-Indian palaces that incorporated elements of Asian and European design. A British lady once remarked that the railway stations were more elegant than many Maharaja palaces. All this, however, for a purpose: to emphasize the glory and power of their rule.

That rule, or raj, was, as in all empires, mortal. In the first half of the twentieth century, the Indians fought for and gained independence in 1947. The world knows the name of Mahatma Gandhi, the father of the liberation movement. Compared to other empires, the British gave away their rule—however grudgingly—with a measure of dignity and fairness.

My father's family was part of that exotic world for almost 200 years; members of my family were in India from 1790 till 1960 and beyond (more on that strange fact later). That world is long gone, and few people know anything about it. Many Americans barely know that there was a British India! Indians might know a little, or want to know less, but some Indians are a little nostalgic about the British era. That fact might sound odd, but I have heard it from the mouths of Indians themselves. The great empire, the proud Raj, has passed on, another footnote in history, for little more than 70 years and largely forgotten.

And irony of ironies: I have lived in an original colony, America, for years. I live right near (less than 20 miles) from where the first English colonists settled in Plymouth, Massachusetts. Since the decline of the British Empire, America has been the dominant force in the world. Somewhat diminished, it is still the great power. In fact, America is a huge empire, once wrestled from the unfortunate American Indians, just as Britain conquered India. And America, despite its faults and errors, has many notable features that have rarely existed elsewhere on this planet: for example, a functioning but limping democracy. I have traveled the planet and studied history, and America, I must say, is unique. Yes, it has its faults, but few countries in history have offered freedom of press and religion, economic opportunity, and democracy.

Even though my father's family lived in India for five generations, I am not an avid fan of the Raj. I am not romantic about that era. The British in India were the ruling class. But like all people, there were notable exceptions and many good people. I see all sides, and today admire the India I see, the India that was once British, and the ancient India that went back thousands of years, with times of great learning, wisdom, and art. Though I was not part of the Vanrenen experience in India, I visited India in 1980 for over four months and marveled at all that I saw. I witnessed incredible poverty and wealth, crowded bustling cities, magical game preserves, stunning buildings and art, and, most of all, the distinct whiff of wisdom hidden here and there. I met a dazzling array of people from all walks of life. I had a great time with my wife, Johnna, in the year just before our son, Gabriel, was born.

There is a poignancy about the passage of time. I look at some of the old photos of my mother and father and see them laughing in their twenties in a beautiful location and think: All that is gone. The moment they lived in that lovely photograph was just a moment, even if precious. At that moment they had breath, life, dreams, and pleasure—the sun on their shoulders, and the air fresh from lake breezes. That moment passed. Now not even a dream. These are not morbid or even sad thoughts: just a wonder at the passage of time and the mystery of life. And most of all a reminder to be grateful for each day; for each morning we get up to face another day; for each friend, obligation, trip to the convenience store, adventure, project, job, and the touch of the hand of your close one. We must not only give a nod to this obligation—we should seize every opportunity to nurture it. This life is a wonderful gift that I now have the maturity to truly appreciate. It is with these thoughts that I embark on the journey of Wally and Zizza, which does not end with their deaths, but continues to this day.

The newlyweds Wally and Zizza at Ysobel's cottage in Gulmarg, a village in the Himalayas, with Granny's many dogs, circa 1939. Slightly out of focus, the photograph was taken at a favorite spot outside the cottage, a location where many other family photos were taken. I can just hear Ysobel, white-haired and dignified, as she gets up from tea, toast, and marmalade at breakfast: "Out you go, all of you, outside, time for a photograph before you leave for Renala." And everyone there, including the dogs, would bustle outside and wait their turn. Yes, a moment in time, a magical moment, but major global changes were rumbling and a terrible war about to commence in Europe. Wally, much to his regret, would soon go overseas to join the battle against Nazi aggression.

TWO

ENGLAND, WHERE IT STARTED

Wally and Zizza's journey starts in England, not too long ago the center of a vast world empire, but which was also, for them, a comfortable world of quaint villages, country roads, farm fields, the little market, and friendly people. As a boy, I knew that world for a short time, and it was, dare I say, magical.

From England, where they married in 1938 at Grandad's antique stone church, they took to the waters, as so many British had done for centuries. It was an island, after all. Centuries ago, the Romans had sailed there and conquered the tribal Celts. England still has Roman ruins, and in the English language many Latin roots. When Rome collapsed, the Romans evacuated England (as the British would do in India in 1947), and Great Britain was once again vulnerable to invaders, and invade they did. In the fifth and sixth centuries AD, Germanic tribes came in waves, conquered, settled, and were Christianized. Amazingly enough, Christianity had come to England at the end of the Roman era and it had flourished. Christianity had an affirmative, civilizing effect on the tough Germanic tribesmen. In the eighth and ninth centuries, England experienced a moderate renaissance, with towns, churches, trade, art, and culture often centered around the Church.

Then another invasion, a huge and scary one: wave upon wave of bearded tough guys from Scandinavia. We call them the Vikings. The Vikings would forcibly settle in eastern regions of England, creating a land of two competing forces: Anglo-Saxon and Scandinavian—a creative ferment, one could say. But in 1066 a typhoon hit Great Britain, a seismic change in every way: the successful invasion of French knights who conquered the Brits at the battle of Hastings, not far from where Zizza was born. The Normans conquered Britain to completion, removing or killing every English duke, judge, or bishop in the top tier of control. Great Britain changed dramatically once it was ruled by a high medieval French culture with knights, priests, and poets. Within several generations, however, the French were absorbed into British culture, and French ceased to be the language of the ruling classes. By the reign of Queen Elizabeth—also the conclusion of Shakespeare's era—England was emerging as a naval power, a trajectory that would soon take them to world empire.

Kent, the region the family is from, faces France, just 30 miles away. Kent, often called the garden of England, has farms, antique villages, history, and architecture: strange Celtic designs on rocks, Roman tile work, medieval castles, Elizabethan houses and gardens, and now, modern highways and towns. Kentish people are imbued with the essence of England: climate, culture, history, and language. And one must not forget the Anglican Church: Each village and town has its stone church, some of them antique, with hymns, Bible reading, and the teachings. For much of its history, the Church and its values had a profound influence on the English. England, in its growth, was not a secular culture, and beneath the dogma of religion lived valuable ideas and values that had an affirmative influence on English people. A question that we must all ask ourselves, in this era of multiple distractions, is what feeds the deep current of my life?

The England that I knew and loved as a little boy still lingers in the country, in the people and in song. As the poet Blake once wrote: *And did those feet in ancient time walk upon this green and pleasant land,* a poem then converted into a rousing church hymn. The Kent images presented in this book show a land bathed in enchantment. That is not my colored glasses; it is in the photographs.

Looking into the past is not just nostalgia or dreaming. It teaches us, for one, to appreciate what we have now, and to live in the present. It helps to show how we are alike in so many ways, not just Europeans but all races, going back to ancient India, Africa, Egypt, and Greece. All lives are enlivened by love, sex, laughter, adventure, jobs, marriage, and children, along with losses, disappointments, disease, and death. We share visions and dreams and we all want to reach out beyond the boundaries, to see what is over the horizon. Sometimes we forget that the limitless horizon is also within.

When Zizza was born February 7, 1919, much of the planet was in turmoil. Does this sound familiar? Europe was recovering from another senseless war that introduced into warfare, for the first time, modern technological inventions: tanks, planes, and poison gases. The horrifying World War I had ended, lasting much longer than the "experts" had predicted, four long bloody years, while on one particularly bad day, thousands of young British men perished in the cold trenches of France. For some inexplicable reason, the powerful countries of Europe—imbued with science and reason—had gone at each other's throats and committed multiple acts of senseless violence. A few call this mass psychosis, a frenzy that afflicts mankind from time to time. We are swayed by our upbringing and environment more than we wish to acknowledge.

Post-war Britain struggled back on its feet, but it was not easy: a new world order, not all good, was emerging. Workers were striking, morale was low, the government struggled, Irish Republicans were restless, a devastating flu epidemic swept the planet, and in India, the beloved and mighty Raj, there were cracks in the seams as Indians began the march to independence. In India, the massacre in Amritsar took place the year Zizza was born, when a British general ordered his "native" troops to fire on an "illegal" gathering in a city square. 379 people died, many more injured before the ten minutes of continuous firing ceased. Even Churchill called this a monstrous act, and many words were exchanged between London and Delhi. Despite all the home and colonial turmoil, Great Britain still managed an empire that spanned the planet. London and its bustling ports, government buildings, and trade was the magnetic center of that great empire.

Only one hour by train from the great capital, Zizza was born in county Kent, which was quiet and rural, far from the agonies and triumphs of empire. As was common in those days, Zizza was born in the house attached to the church, but they would soon move to Smeeth Rectory (her father, Alan Bruce Ronald, the village minister). His ancestors came from Ayrshire, Scotland, where the family farm, The Benals, still stands. Many of the Ronalds shipped out to Australia and developed a lucrative wool empire with banks, farms, and factories. Alan Bruce, however, was a spiritual man who eschewed business and embraced his role as pastor to his village.

Alan Bruce with his wife, Eileen—in the hat—and two of their daughters in front. Sarah is on the left, and Zizza holds a doll, on the right. Smack center is the indomitable Miss Moisey, the governess. Her central position is no accident. Mommy was a shy, anxious

woman and daddy a gentle, somewhat absent-minded father. Miss Moisey was known
for her bossy manner and endless aphorisms, many which I learnt—with much laughter
on both sides—from Zizza. If you didn't finish your dinner you were told: "Beggars can't
be choosers," or on another night it might be "Waste not, want not." It is quite remarkable,
and no accident, the central position Miss Moisey holds in the photograph.

Alan Bruce had graduated from Cambridge University and was appointed reverend of the quiet little parish in pastoral Kent. He was softly spoken, with a thick head of brown hair swept back, a gentle poetic face, and held a fine reputation in his village. His favorite authors were Ralph Waldo Emerson and Saint Paul. Although they lived close to the most important city on the planet, their village was a world apart, as if some fairy godmother had swept her wand over the county: quaint, sleepy, humble, and countrified.

The rectory had a vegetable garden, chickens, and a field out back. Mr. Ames, with his stoop and white moustache, would drop by every day to tend the garden and chickens. He would smile and wave: Good morning to you, Mam, a fine day it is. The children, four girls and one boy, would be tended by a governess until old enough to attend the local school in tidy blue and white uniforms. Miss Moisey, a minor legend in our family, was a dour but dedicated governess bristling with aphorisms to conquer every weakness on this planet.

On Saturday, the children would walk the few hundred yards to the sweetie shop to indulge themselves. There was a greengrocer in town, Mr. Andrews, who would be open six days a week to offer everything the local gardens could not. Every day for fifty years, he would wear his green apron, tie, white shirt, and his gum (rubber) boots. Almost everyone attended church on Sunday to listen to "Daddy's" sermon, usually inspired by Saint Paul, and there would be hymns and Sunday lunch after. Only years later would I appreciate the courage and wisdom of St Paul, a major force in the growth of Christianity.

There were few cars at that time, no highway, no convenience store, and few phones. If you were lucky enough to own a phone, they were primitive, working through an overburdened operator. Long-distance calls were a challenge. Radios were still being developed. Everyone knew everyone, gossip was rife but gentle, and many used a Raleigh bicycle. For entertainment, there was the cinema in Ashford, but only on Saturdays, local church dances, and strolls in the countryside. Cinema was mostly British films (BBC), often quite good, but sometimes romantic fluff or nationalistic battles. Occasionally, there would be a joyous trek to the closest beach, and from that beach one could look across to the dim outline of France from where the battered troops had recently returned.

The two young sisters Sarah and Zizza—on the left—in their English country world, distant from the seething world outside, and between two world wars. Their life still had the tinge of the Victorian era, though that had formally ended with the death of Queen Victoria in 1901. This remarkable woman was the longest-reigning monarch in British history, ruling during the peak of British achievement in art, science, and world exploration.

Even though England was the center of a world empire, the people of the countryside were modest, gentle, and kind, and many of the rural villages looked like something out of a BBC movie: quaint, clean, and old-fashioned, with few cars, no major highways, no malls, no gas stations, and no advertising on the side of roads. Everything was clean and organic: the houses and villages and farms were formed like a single organism after centuries of careful observation. People had affirmative values that made for a good life. They were honest, hard-working, and kind to others, and displayed little of the corruption and selfishness that sometimes afflicts people not grounded in sensible values.

It was a simple life, not perfect of course, with all the problems and troubles people always have, but yet quite innocent. The English of the countryside were not snobs; they were down-to-earth people who were honest and kind, often hospitable and caring—like many country people in any time or place.

"Daddy," Zizza's father, Reverend Alan Bruce Ronald. He had a remarkable life, born into the Victorian era, the twelfth of thirteen children, and son to a prosperous wool merchant. As a young adventurer, he would spend a few years as a missionary in the wilderness of far West Canada, but after living through a Canadian winter in a cabin, he returned to England. His wife, for one, was not going to live in a wilderness. Scholar and lover of fine literature and the best of Christian writing, he would live out his life as the beloved vicar of a bucolic English village.

Zizza had, for those days, a moderately-sized family: mother (Eirene) and her father; one boy, David—Mommy's favorite—and Rachel, Mary, Zizza, and Sarah. It is interesting to note that after they grew up, they all looked different and had lives that were not at all alike. For example, Rachel, whom I remember well, became the wife of a modest farmer north of London. When I was 14 I visited and was charmed by her, the farm house—with no central heating, refrigerator, or showers (only baths)—and the animals. She was tall, kind, and modest, with a stately bearing, as if she had been born into royalty, and she had one jolly son, Nicholas, with whom I still correspond.

David, the only boy in the Ronald family, lived an exciting life, retiring as a Colonel in NATO after years of distinguished service. As a boy, I met him only briefly, and recall the sweat I suffered when he asked me to polish his leather army boots. I had never encountered such attention to detail, but he was a cheerful uncle, confident and friendly. All the siblings shared a zest for life.

From a distance, one can romanticize their world, but we all know that no time or people live without blind spots, troubles, and struggles. Still, the family showed all the signs of health and happiness, and all five children would survive into adulthood, prosper, marry, and have children. Their generation would see the decline and end of the great empire, and they would experience two world wars and the amazing rebirth in the 1950s of economy and culture, ushering in the buoyant era of the Beatles! And across the Atlantic Ocean, the rise of the mighty engine of America, a country that would surpass Britain as the world power.

In Zizza's early years, England existed in a different world. Everyone was embedded in the fact of being English, sharing a common history, language, religion, and values. They all, in different ways, were aware that their tiny island nation governed a mighty empire that ruled the seven seas with its navy. They all read the empire news in the local papers; in the national magazines that came to the little "news" shop; and in the books, romantic and historical. There was nationalistic propaganda in all those books, novels, and comics,

The four Ronald girls with their mother and friend. Zizza, an innocent, happy ten-year-old, is on the right in front. An idyllic summer day in Kent, circa 1929, four years before the ascendancy of Hitler. Then life would change drastically, but in 1929 the day was warm, the picnic relaxing, and even mummy had a good time. Eirene, as I understand, was often anxious and always hiding under a big hat.

Daddy's church—as Zizza would say—Smeeth rectory. The photograph was sent to me by Sheila, my Ronald cousin, taken when she revisited Smeeth.

Alan Bruce sitting on the right next to his shy wife, Eirene; David next to Mary in back; Rachel standing on the left next to an unidentified lady. Funny, a name just came to me, perhaps true: Aunt Hilda. Life was good, house and garden comfortable and very close to "daddy's" church. One could walk down to the village market and sweetie shop, and the family employed a cook, gardener, and a governess.

and in school. History books told the stories with embellishment: the great Captain Cook who explored the Pacific and was speared to death on the shores of Hawaii; famous generals in India; and thrilling exploits from remote corners of the globe. Often there were exciting tales of brave cavalry men in India fighting dark-skinned bad guys. In Kent, they all felt a vague pride about this, but it did not really change daily life very much. Between the wars, life in Smeeth went on at its slow, gentle pace, seemingly unfazed by the big world.

Kent, in Zizza's youth, was blessed with an aura of magic that permeated that gentle green rolling land filled with stories and legends. It is an exceptionally beautiful region: mild weather, stone farm houses, and the thick cover of trees, grasses, and flowers. Even today one can feel it. In fact, all the region south of London from Dorset to Kent shares this ambience. And what a history, with many stories: Thomas Hardy, Charles Darwin, Lewis Carroll, William Blake (the poet), and many others resided in the region south of London. Something in that ambience is captured in the song and stories of the region. Somewhere to the west of Smeeth, Alice fell down the rabbit hole. And what better place to experience it than *Winnie the Pooh*, the much-loved children's story. The forest that inspired the tales of Christopher Robin and Pooh, the adorable bear, is down the road from Smeeth.

This is a picture of sleepy New Romney—not far from Zizza's village of Smeeth—where Wally's family had a family home. They kept a house in England as well as Renala, their farm/estate in India. New Romney, a pretty village near the English Channel, is famous for the Romney marshes and beautiful country walks near the waters. Nearly 90 years old, this photograph depicts a world that has almost vanished. You can find traces here and there, but mostly in the remote places of Scotland, Cornwall, or Wales.

This house, called Martinfield, near New Romney, Kent is where the "Indian" Vanrenens kept an English home. In reality, the Vanrenens, including my father, spent little time in Martinfield, except on an occasional trip home, or during the holidays in their teen years when they were interned in boarding schools, to be indoctrinated into British values and empire propaganda.

Wally's soccer team at Clifton College. Wally is seated on the far right. Many of these boys would have already lost a father or uncle in World War I, and many would go on to fight in World War II. These two major wars would deeply affect the lives of all these boys and their families. All these lads were fully ingrained into their role as young empire boys, already with ambitions to serve in Africa or India. Wally is not the only English lad there whose parents lived far away in India. He was a stranger in England, perhaps a stranger in India. In his years as a student in England, I do not know how many times he returned to India—the journey was at least a one-month round trip. For most of the year, he was separated from his parents. He is about fourteen years old in this photo, and looks mature, thoughtful and, perhaps, sad. In the photograph, one can see that each boy unwittingly displays something true about themselves in their expression and posture.

None of these boys could guess that their world and fate would soon change radically. Across the channel, in Munich, Germany, a former street artist and corporal in the German army was attracting followers in taverns. For effect, the charismatic dynamo sported a little moustache. Germany, weary and disgruntled after World War I, was gearing up for a brush with national psychosis. In actuality, the whole of Europe, including England, would have a brush with grave stupidity. Today, we make the common mistake, blaming "the other," not looking into our own world and hearts.

Wally attended Clifton College (in photograph above), which in America we would call a preparatory school. Clifton, set in elegant stone buildings on a lovely campus, still prospers in the city of Bristol. Why did Wally go there? Clifton, in the empire days, was a training ground for boys planning a colonial career. Rugby, cricket, running, and soccer were popular at Clifton, and the classics, Greek and Roman, were emphasized. All students were indoctrinated in the key role that Britain had to play in history. It was taught that Britain's greatness derived from its Greco-Roman heritage. Do not forget to read your Cicero and Caesar! In Latin! It was a disciplined world with a tight schedule, sports every afternoon, and the compulsory school uniform. In the morning after a common breakfast at long wooden tables, there would be a general gathering with hymns, announcements, and the headmaster's speech. In the evening after a formal dinner in the large dining hall, there were two hours of quiet homework. Then a short break, time to brush teeth, followed by bedtime–quiet. Discipline was quick, sometimes harsh.

I was pleased to discover that the stellar comedian, John Cleese of Monty Python, graduated from Clifton. In his autobiography, one can see a picture of the young Cleese in his uniform in front of these very buildings! Cleese would become a master of making fun of the stuffy British mannerisms, some of which he picked up at Clifton. The school was also a training ground for musicians and artists: Michael Redgrave, Trevor Howard, and other respected actors would attend this school.

After Clifton, Wally attended the Royal Military Academy, Sandhurst, the British equivalent to West Point. He was destined to train as an officer for the British Indian army, but he once told me that he regretted not going to Cambridge University like his brother, John. In his essence, Wally liked farming and learning; he loved to write and read and kept a journal many years of his life. He was born into a military family, and in those days, expectations were often fixed, but his heart was not really in soldiering. His two sons, living in America, would have a chance to find their own way.

Old postcards from the late 1920s depicting the ambience of New Romney and Kent. It seems like (well, it was) another world and century. High Street in New Romney does not have a moving car or truck and seems eerily quiet.

A sweet photograph of a specific moment in time that is now long gone: Five teenagers on a French beach in summer, around 1931. Wally is in the middle with glasses. To the right is his brother, John and sister Hazel, who holds a little camera. The cocky young man who stares at the camera is someone who would get used to being photographed. In fact, he made a career in the movies. He is Trevor Howard, who would go on to become a famous actor, starring in some excellent British movies. His most memorable movie is a David Lean classic about a man and women who meet on a train (Brief Encounter). They feel a love for each other, but in the end decide not to pain their respective families. It is very British.

Wally and Trevor became friends at Clifton College. Like Wally, Trevor came from a colonial family, his father working far away in Sri Lanka, and, for a time, the wandering Trevor was happy to attach himself to my father's family. Trevor, interestingly enough, would specialize in cinema as steely, gruff British army officers. A heavy drinker who fought in World War II, he was well suited for those roles.

To the left of Trevor is Doris, Wally's other sister. Hazel would be the go-getter, charming and attractive; Wally the intense handsome one; John, adventurous and easy-going; and Doris, the shy, vulnerable sister. The foursome was tight in those glorious youthful days and shared many adventures. They called themselves "The Four." Trevor fit right in to make, for that summer, a comfortable Five.

When Wally was 24, he returned to England for a visit, staying at the family home, Martinfield, in Kent. As was common in those days, the church dance was where you might meet a pretty lady. And this was perhaps the purpose of his trip "home." A "good" family would not encourage their children to socialize in taverns or pubs. A church dance was where one could find the right ladies. It was at a particular dance in sunny May where he met a charming, cheerful young lady from a neighboring village in Kent. She was a tall brunette, a little shy but prone to smiles and laughter. Their courtship did not last long: Wally had a boat to India to catch!

In a flash, Zizza emerged from the magical little kingdom of Kent and entered the big and strange world. One sunny Sunday, walking on the bluffs over the blue channel, Wally proposed to Zizza, who was most flattered and pleased to become his fiancée. He was handsome and debonair, a young Indian cavalry officer, and there were thrilling stories about his family in India, which seemed like something out of a fabulous book: sleek race horses, palm trees, tigers, and tales of heroism and valor. Everyone in England marveled at tales and descriptions of India.

Wally and Zizza are off to the continent for a honeymoon, before the journey to a new life in India. This was a monumental transition for my mother, but the newlyweds are happy, very happy, and together they welcome this new life, and all it will bring. It was, however, a precarious time, and as the cliché goes: storm clouds on the horizon—1938! Their honeymoon was a jaunt to France and Paris, a perennial favorite then and now for many in my family.

RECTOR'S DAUGHTER WEDS AT BIDDENDEN

Lieut. W. D. Vanrenen And Miss E. A. Ronald

[illegible] Elizabeth Anne Ronald, third daughter [illegible] of the Rev. A. B. Ronald, the [illegible] of Biddenden, and of Mrs. Ronald, was married at Biddenden parish church on Thursday [illegible]. The bridegroom was Lieut. Walter Den[illegible] Vanrenen, of the Central India Horse, [illegible] who is the elder son of Mrs. [illegible] Vanrenen, of Re[illegible] Estate, Punjab, India

and of Martinfield, New Romney, and of the late Major Denys Henry Vanrenen.

The Venerable T. K. Sopwith, Archdeacon of Maidstone, conducted the ceremony. The bride was given away by her father.

Miss Ronald wore a beautiful gown of white and gold embossed satin with a white tulle secured by a wreath of orange blossom. Her bouquet was of lilies.

The bridesmaids were Miss Doris Vanrenen (bridegroom's sister) and Miss Sarah Ronald, sister of the bride. Both wore gowns of delphinium coloured chiffon and carried bouquets of blue delphiniums.

Count F. von Pongracz was the best man.

The church was beautifully decorated with blue delphiniums, the favourite flowers of the bride. The choral service opened with the singing of "Praise, my soul, the King of Heaven," by the parish church choir and concluded with the hymn "Glorious things of Thee are spoken," and the Wedding March.

After the service, which was attended by Ministers of many neighbouring parishes, a reception was held at the Rectory. The bride and bridegroom later left for the Continent. For travelling, the bride wore a navy, white-striped silk frock with hat and coat to match.

A cablegram of congratulations from Lord and Lady Brabourne was received from India.

The bridegroom's gift to the bride was his regimental brooch in diamonds and platinum. Officers of the Central India Horse sent a silver tray.

This tattered article from a local English paper in 1938 announces their wedding: Elizabeth Anne Ronald marries Lieut. Vanrenen of Central India Horse, she from Kent, he from Renala Estate, Punjab, India. She the daughter of Alan Bruce Ronald, and Eirene, he the oldest son of Major Denys Henry, and his wife Ysobel, (both also from Martinfield, New Romney, Kent.) Miss Ronald wore a beautiful gown of white and gold embossed satin with white tulip secured by a wreath of orange blossoms. Her bouquet was of lilies. The bridesmaid was Miss Doris Vanrenen (bridegrooms' sister) and Sarah Ronald, sister of the bride, and both wore gowns of delphinium colored chiffon and carried bouquet of blue delphiniums. The venerable T. K. Sopwith, Archdeacon of Maidstone, conducted the ceremony. The bride was given away by her father. The church was beautifully decorated with beautiful delphiniums. Count F. (Freddie) Von Pongacz was the best man. The choral service opened with singing "Praise my soul, the king of Heaven," *and concluded with* "Glorious Things of Thee are spoke," *and the* "Wedding March." *After the reception in the rectory, the bride and bridegroom left for the continent. For traveling, the bride wore a navy, white-striped silk frock with hat and coat to match. A telegram had arrived from India from Lord and Lady Braebourne. The bridegroom's gift to the bride was his regimental brooch in diamonds and platinum. Officers of the Central India Horse sent a silver tray!*

The great wedding day, Wally and Zizza smiling in the center. Doris Vanrenen, Wally's sister, is on the left, next to her husband, Len Mitchell, of the Mitchell Estates in the Punjab—a near neighbor to Renala. Today, this estate still operates in Pakistan (under, of course, a different ownership). I just enjoyed some Mitchell farms Mango chutney. I purchased this product, amazingly enough, at an Indian grocery just south of Boston. On the right are Sarah Ronald, Zizza's younger sister, and her husband, Tony Scrace. Sarah, who worked intelligence during and after the war, would meet Tony Scrace in India.

THREE

INDIA, HOW DID THAT HAPPEN?

Zizza's early life, living in an enchanted region with a close family, was very English. Wally, however, was born in another world, thousands of miles away in India, at a time when travel was strictly by ship. The journey from England to India could take three weeks one way. Wally was five years old when Zizza was born in 1919, having spent his early years at the family estate in India, called Renala.

His father, Denys Henry, an army officer, raised horses for the British Indian army in an age when horses were of great importance in civilian and military life. In a few years, Wally would be shipped off to the mother country to receive an education at a British school to train him to be a proper English gentleman.

Wally and Zizza could have been born on different planets. Wally's family lived in a tropical Asian nation ruled precariously by a British government whose might depended on the British Indian army. His family were privileged military/landowner class who lived a life of hard work amidst the trappings of luxury. Wally's home at Renala was a grand old colonial building—inside like a British country home— surrounded by lovely tropical gardens in a circle of farms and fields and horse paddocks. The Vanrenen home, embellished with fine furniture and Asian art, was supported by a small army of Indians: cooks, gardeners, butlers, and on the outside, numerous farm workers.

As a young boy, his closest friend beside his mother, beloved Ysobel, might have been the Ayah, the Indian equivalent to the nanny. Every English boy and girl had their Ayah from whom they learned the sounds and tales of this strange and wondrous nation. Years later, they would remember the Ayah. She would sing songs in Hindi or Urdu, tell stories, and often sleep outside the door of the little sahib or memsahib. The little ones could not help but be influenced by the sights and sounds of great India, the many Indian people in and around the house, the tropical flowers and birds, the frightening tales of cobras and tigers, and the terrible heat of summer when all could be heard but the buzzing of insects. Daddy was often away, and when home brusque and busy, but at the short family gatherings, maybe at Christmas, they would exchange presents, enjoy hot chocolate and British candies, and sing familiar hymns around the drooping Christmas tree, surrounded, of course, by the household staff who also participated in the festivities.

One can see the little boy and his brother, John, wandering the grounds and adjacent barns and fields, admiring the handsome horses that looked so big. The local Indian workers would stop to smile and chat with the little British boys. Perhaps the horses would be grazing in a paddock, or lodged in the barns, and best of all taken out for a ride by one of the grown-ups. It was customary for the young boys to be given riding lessons on ponies. They lived like little princes in a little kingdom. One could even say it was magical, removed from the vast spaces and cramped towns of India, and all the concerns of politics and nation.

But it was a precarious miniature kingdom, a tiny part of the vast exotic nation of India, which was filled with many kinds of people and places. A land, too, that was occupied. The year Zizza was born, 1919, Wally was five, and not far from Renala the British had a skirmish with Afghanistan, called the third Afghani war. This dirty little war was a cry of frustration from the Afghanis, who were tired of British meddling. It ended with a flat victory for the mighty British, but the Afghanis had made their point. Uncle Louis and my grandfather had roles in this conflict, the third of its kind. The first war, in the early 1840s, was a tragedy for the British: They lost a whole army in the Khyber Pass, one of their most disastrous defeats in the history of the empire. Many of those who died were starved, shot, or frozen. Many of these were women and children known as camp followers. None of these were honored later. No one has subdued Afghanistan for long; no one, one would think, would be so foolish as to try. But empires have a life of their own and an imperative to maintain power over a large area of land for as long as possible. How strange that America has troops there now!

Wally's little childhood idyll would not last long. As soon as the boys were six or seven, they would board the big ocean liner for the long voyage home. They would return to that distant second home, their family house called Martinfield in County Kent. They would then be packed off to the boarding school where they would live most of the year. That strict regimen, so far from Renala and their parents, would go on until graduation, when they were sixteen or seventeen. From then it was more schooling: Wally would attend the military college of Sandhurst, the West Point of England, and his brother, John, would matriculate at the venerable Cambridge University. Both would return as young men to serve in India in the cavalry. This, of course, was expected.

In 1938, however, a great event transpired that changed everything. Wally would bring a bride back to Renala and India. After the wedding, the second big jump in Wally and Zizza's amazing journey was the ocean liner voyage through the Mediterranean to India, the start of a long and exciting segment of their married lives. A young and naïve Zizza, rector's daughter from an English village, was whisked off to India by her debonair British Indian husband, an officer in the elite British Indian cavalry.

Their first journey together, however, was no ordinary trip: They journeyed on a British ship through the Mediterranean, to the Suez

Canal in Egypt, and then on to the Red Sea, on their way across the Indian Ocean to the great port of Bombay. They fraternized with fellow passengers in the dining room, complete with uniformed waiters and white table cloths; they danced to a live band in the evenings; and during the day played games on the decks. Reaching the Suez Canal, they were exposed to a very different world, Asia. People looked radically different, palm trees lined the canal, and the air was sticky and hot; it sounded different, and the aromas in the air were foreign. As you looked over the banister as the ship squeezed through the long canal—on its way to the Indian Ocean—you could see and hear the Arab hawkers, the lines of camels, and the desert hills in the distance. Not far away were the great pyramids.

As in all the unexpected turns in life that we all share, Wally would return to Egypt in a few years during the conflict with the Germans. He would captain a secret unit that would penetrate the mysterious highlands of Ethiopia in a successful attempt to undermine the Italians. Mussolini, in his absurd ambitions to emulate the British Empire, had colonized Ethiopia, in those days one of the most remote countries on our planet. Wally never told me any stories about the war.

Zizza and Wally's adventurous journey had begun, a circuitous path that would take them to India, Renala, the Himalayas for holidays, and on to many other exotic places for the next fifty years. They would experience much turmoil and discomfort as their life—and world— changed and as their circumstances shifted, but also much adventure and happiness.

Wally, on left, receiving a prize at a horse race, about 1937 in Lahore, India. Wally was also an avid polo player during his stint in the British Indian cavalry. The cups were always handed over by some important lady! She would inevitably be the wife of the local leading politician, Lord so and so, and she would smile at Wally: "Jolly good show, Captain Vanrenen." He would smile and shake her hand. "Ah," she would add, "you were here last year, were you not?" He would nod. "I do hope you come to gala tonight."

FOUR

HOW DID THE BRITISH END UP IN INDIA?

Why did Wally and Zizza go to this distant Asian nation for the first decade of their marriage? The simple answer is that Wally's family was what was then called British Indian, which in the old days meant an English person who lived in India. How did this happen? And how did Wally's father, Denys Henry, end up pioneering a horse farm in a remote corner of that huge country? This estate and farm, at its height famous for its horses, would be called Ren-ala. I can only think that Ysobel, my grandmother, would have come up with that quixotic name.

Renala existed in the great Punjab province of India; to the northwest, about three hours by car, one reaches the imposing entrance to the infamous Khyber Pass—the gateway to India— and the rough country of Afghanistan. Afghanistan has always been a troubled country: extremely mountainous and bristling with hostile tribes, but also rich in human and cultural interests. Afghanis are no ordinary tribes; rather, their fierce warriors have been hardened by centuries of intertribal rivalries and the passage of foreign armies.

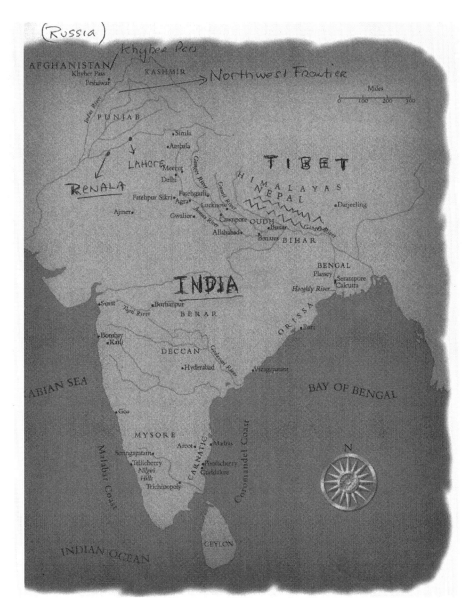

The above map shows the relative location of Renala in India. Today, Renala would be in the modern nation of Pakistan.

In the 1930s and 1940s, Hollywood produced adventure movies about this region, one even called the *Khyber Pass*. For a time, this Northwest Frontier, adjacent to Afghanistan and near Renala, fascinated and frustrated the British. The region played a major role in the life of my family: Many relatives, including my great Uncle, were posted on the Frontier. Renala came into being because the British army needed good, strong horses for the dangerous border patrols. This was in the era when horses were paramount in policing and war.

Lahore, one of the great cities of Asia, is the nearest city to Renala, and today this bustling crossroads is the cultural capital of Pakistan. As you go east from Lahore, you travel on one of the major roads in Asia into India, not too far from the capital, New Delhi. Pakistan and India, however, are not and never have been on friendly terms. Pakistan emerged as an independent Muslim nation following independence from British rule. India was thus rudely divided, and the tragedy of this partition rocketed around the world, as millions were displaced and thousands killed.

Lahore, so important for my family, is filled with impressive buildings and grand hotels; it is rich in culture and history, and today filled with malls, banks, highways, sport stadiums, and markets. One thing that the Pakistani people inherited from the British is a love for field hockey and cricket, and in Lahore one can find many sporting fields and complexes. But Lahore is much else: beautiful mosques, historical palaces, lovely gardens, museums, crowded streets and markets, and faded remnants of the British Raj: government buildings, libraries, and gardens.

Today Lahore, with all the hustle and noise of a modern Asian city, is the main tourist attraction of Pakistan. The Sufis, the gentle mystics of Islam, have had positive influence on Lahore, indeed the whole region, and to this day one can hear the captivating devotional songs of the Qawwali singers, who made a splash in world music in the past decades. In the region, there are many shrines to Sufi saints that the locals honor every day. Taliban people, often coming from outside, are the aggressive dualists who have destroyed some of these shrines. They represent the extreme of Islam, if one can even call them Islamic. Dualists, of whatever race, religion, or intellectual system, see the world as me and them, good and evil, positive and negative.

Lahore is strategically located on one of the tributaries of the great Indus, the major river of Pakistan, and one of the most formidable rivers of the world with more volume of water than the Nile. Coming down from the Himalayas through central Pakistan and emptying out into the Indian Ocean, it is the central feature of Pakistan and provides water, irrigation, energy, and beauty. Renala was built near a tributary that leads into the great Indus.

The British engineered a complex system of canals throughout the Punjab that enabled farms to expand and grow. Renala, and many Indian farmers, benefited from this brilliant engineering work.

Curiously, south of Renala is one of the great archaeological sites of the Indian subcontinent: the ruins of a vanished civilization, Harrapo. A mysterious spot, these ruins speak of former—over 2,000 years ago—cultural achievements. Little is known about this Indus River civilization that flourished around the time of the great pharaohs, but the remains of the street blocks, buildings, and a plumbing system point to a people who were advanced and learned.

Someone once called Lahore a great survivor. Few cities exist in such a pathway of trade, commerce, change, and conquest. Situated on route to the Khyber Pass, Lahore is the gateway city to the rich plains of the huge Indian subcontinent. It is also a major city in the prosperous state of the Punjab, always a vigorous region for politics, money, industry, and farms as well as roving invaders, traders, and conquerors. The great Alexander came into this region—in fact, halted here in his westward path of conquest. Tamerlane troops blasted through, as well as warriors related to Genghis Khan; Muslim armies repeatedly erupted from Central Asia; and always, there were Afghani bandits, warriors, and traders.

A tourist, Johnna, in front of one of the great Muslim palaces, the Red Fort in Agra. In the fourteenth century, a new breed of invader slipped though the dangerous passes of Afghanistan, hearing rumors about great cities, farmland, and the wealth of the Punjab. Like so many before them, they could not resist: furthermore, they were fired by the passions of their faith: it was not just plunder. This new Muslim rule was called the Mughals, and this is where we get the word mogul!

The Mughal government set up an efficient means of administration over a large area, which required armies, taxes, officials, and civil servants—as well as the mullahs. Forts, palaces, government buildings, as well as lush gardens, were erected all over the Punjab and beyond. Paintings, buildings, crafts, and gardens reached an astonishing peak of beauty and harmony.

It was in this grandiose era that one of the planet's loveliest buildings was erected, the famed Taj Mahal, which attracts up to 8,000,000 tourists a year. I was lucky to visit the Taj, and what impressed me the most is this: It is made of glistening white marble inlaid with semi-precious stone, and from a distance the building is a majestic jewel, but if one comes very close, eyes a few feet from the marble walls, one is astonished to see the level of the craftsmanship, each square foot a work of art, inlaid stones in delicate patterns in the marble. And this on a building whose main dome is ten stories high. It is said that 20,000 artisans from all over Asia, and even Italy, worked for ten years, helped by over 1,000 elephants. Shah Jahan, the emperor of the time, was a man with a remarkable vision—assisted by his Sufi wise men—driven by a wish to honor his beloved wife who had died in childbirth.

At the end of the sixteenth century, the Mughals reached their zenith with a ruler called Akbar. Akbar's armies conquered almost the whole of India, a stunning accomplishment in a time before fast roads and electric communication. The Muslim Mughals, a minority in a Hindu world, established a new power throughout India, one of great accomplishment, art, building, and, often, a measure of fairness to all people.

The Mughals, at their peak, realized that they should not mismanage the very people they had conquered. Leaders like Akbar employed Hindus in his armies and government. But despite the veneer of incredible wealth, art, and buildings, most of India was poor and peasant, and life could be extremely hard and uncertain for the common person. Mughals, like so many dominant classes in history, could be violent and cruel. Traitors or criminals were buried or burned alive; mass slaughter was not uncommon; and people, without the sword of power, were weak and helpless. Still, the Mughals had a run of effective power where the region, if not the country, was marked by periods of peace, creativity, and prosperity. An intolerant, self-indulgent ruling class never produces works of outstanding intelligence and art. A ruling class dominated by dualism is usually cruel, self-serving, and short-lived. The Mughals, for a time, displayed a lively spirit and much achievement on the earthly plane.

The greatest gem of Mughal art, the Taj Mahal. When you see this building in person, you will experience feelings that few buildings in the world will evoke. Even the foundation is an astonishing work of engineering, as the building has not only survived four centuries, but it has barely shifted. In the great Muslim architecture and art, one sees an admirable reverence for the wonder of creation. This building does not only speak of man's achievement: it is, somehow, beyond ego and time.

FIVE

AKBAR AND THE MOGHULS AND EUROPEAN EXPANSION

Anyone who wants to understand British India, and the Vanrenen presence there, needs to glance at the fabulous story of the Moghul Empire, which preceded British rule.

Around 1600, there was a great ferment of change in the world, stemming from an energetic and expanding Europe. In fact, a seismic change was already in motion—these years were a major pivot in European and world history. Europe had marched into a vigorous era of exploration, scientific study, and world trade. Queen Elizabeth, who helped launch England into a world power, died in 1602. Akbar died in 1605, and around 1612, the British first landed on Indian shore, a modest landfall of small wooden ships with men who looked in amazement at the reality of tropical and ancient India. They were the first ominous messengers of a new era; their intentions were not all good.

Europe, in the grips of a renaissance of learning, science, and technology, was bursting at the seams, eager to map the planet to dominate it for trade and colonization. This was the century of world exploration: British, French, Portuguese, Spanish, and Dutch—all competing viciously with each other—would travel the oceans in search of new lands and new wealth.

The dam had been opened and there was no stopping it. In 1620, seemingly innocuous, humble pilgrims landed in Plymouth Harbor in what would become the great state of Massachusetts. They were the flag bearers of a coming onslaught of Europeans who would soon push the American Indians aside.

Meantime, in India, the Moghuls were living in their fairy kingdom, both good and evil, far removed from the realities of Europe and the renaissance of science, navigation, guns, and knowledge. Akbar was born into privilege and from an early age trained to be a ruler: emperor, king, and supreme person with the power of life and death. Akbar, unlike many autocrats, used his power wisely. He was a remarkable man and a great leader. He was a talented hunter and warrior, a brilliant and inspiring general, and a generous and visionary leader. Akbar, let us emphasize, was Islamic, influenced by a conservative class of clerics who were intensely protective of their religion. But Akbar was also a unique and open-minded man, open to the influence of the gentle mystics of Islam (the Sufis). Mystics, everywhere, are alike—of whatever culture of religion: There is One, all united, common to all. What we call the One is up to our place and preference. No one owns this One, but all can come into contact with it because they are a part of it. What separates, or creates duality, is our own limitation in thought and feeling.

To this day the Sufis are active in the region, including Pakistan, and contribute much in the way of art, music, and tolerance to their people. They do not live their Islam from rigid dogma, that is from a stagnant "two"; this dualism–of whatever faith, or no faith–is what creates division, suspicion, and aggression. Sufis are devout, often enhancing their spirituality with contemplation, discussion, song, and holy dance. Sufi shrines and monuments to their saints can be found all over Pakistan, Afghanistan, and Lahore. The more reactionary types—the dualists—like the Taliban, often despise the more tolerant Sufis and even destroy their shrines.

These open-hearted people have always existed in all religions, but in Akbar's day—and this very moment—the reactionaries (the dualists) were active and corrosively influential. Akbar, however, enjoyed and encouraged discourse in his court. He was curious about the ideas and beliefs of Christianity and other religions and would invite foreign priests (including Jesuits) to his court to engage in talk. His more conservative clerics frowned on his liberal attitudes. Akbar, however, went a little further: He is said to have claimed that there is one God for all people. In fact, Akbar wanted to be a prophet of a universal faith. Akbar's favorite saint, Chisti, was a Sufi holy man, and his yearnings went beyond that of his more conventional clerics. Akbar built a capital near this man's abode, Fatepur Sikri, which was abandoned because water became scarce. Today, this haunting palace is an intriguing tourist site: an abandoned Mughal complex of incredible beauty—preserved by isolation and desert.

When he died in 1605, Akbar left a kingdom that was strong and united. His son Janghir rose to the occasion, but neither he nor anyone else who followed ever matched the grandeur of Akbar's reign. Janghir, even with his fondness for drugs, luxury, and harem, maintained the vigor of the Mughals. His reign was marked by a great event: the visit in 1615 of a proper English diplomat, not some sea captain, soldier, or trader. Queen Elizabeth, a vigorous and talented leader, wished to direct her young nation to new levels of wealth, exploration, trade, and power. She encouraged the nascent East India Company to flex its muscles—in time to become one of the most powerful trading companies on the planet. They needed permission from the Mughal emperor to trade in India, and they needed to sneak under the noses of the jealous and possessive Portuguese, who already controlled a few small trading posts on India shores.

The British, Dutch, and Portuguese were fierce rivals for the great goods of India: valuable spices, silk, cotton, dyes, and opium. Let us not forget that opium was one of the few effective pain relievers, and that spices–which did not grow in Europe—were extremely valuable for culinary and medical purposes: ginger, cardamom, pepper, turmeric, and more. If you, as a British sea captain, were able to return to England—through storms, pirates, and foreign attacks—with a load of Indian spices, you had hit the jackpot. You could be fabulously wealthy, and all those stock holders who footed the bill—they would be very happy. Yes, there was the science of discovery and exploration, the thrill of adventure, but the bottom line was money.

In 1602, when Queen Elizabeth died, James the First became king of England, now a rising nation in an increasingly aggressive Europe. He, like Queen Elizabeth, encouraged Eastern trade and pushed Sir Thomas Roe east. Thomas Roe was a lord and armed with a letter from the king of England. It took Roe two months to get to Surat, the tiny European foothold on the huge Indian subcontinent. It took him several months to settle into the hostile environment—the Portuguese did their best to halt his progress. It took him some time to get permission from the emperor to travel to the Mughal capital for a visit. It took him more than six weeks to get to that capital, in a foreign world with oppressive heat, strange customs, and often precarious events—disease, bandits, surly Portuguese, suspicious Muslims, and a vast mass of bewildered people who had never seen an English entourage travel through their world.

The ever-patient (and sturdy) Roe—who refused to loosen his attire—would, in time, meet the gracious emperor—whom he called an affable and intelligent man. Jahangir was polite but was not very interested in the letter from an unknown king from a "little" country on the other side of the planet. Jahangir allowed Roe and his entourage to "hang out" for some time, feted by fine dinners, music, dancing girls, and all the paraphernalia of an extravagant court. His visit, amazingly enough, turned into several years. Roe and his entourage had entered a land of riches, fable, and art that was truly astonishing—but they did want to return home! The luxury, gardens, art, and comfort of the Mughal palaces were something out of *Arabian Nights*, but there was an undercurrent of danger and intrigue. A renegade prince could be butchered alive with his companions and wives.

Persistent Thomas Roe never succeeded in getting the emperor to sign a special treaty with England, but he succeeded in much more. He was, it is true, granted some trade concessions, but what he, and all his colleagues, opened was far beyond what he or Jahangir could imagine. Jahangir, his court, indeed his country, had no idea what was brewing in Europe: a new breed of men, a vigorous society armed with new kinds of weapons, traveling on sleek, fast ships bristling with cannons, and motivated by a passion for learning—but money, once again, was the burning fuel. The medieval Mughal Empire, indeed all the countries of Asia, Africa, and South America, were living in an antiquated world that had many traditions, charms, natural resources, and beauty, but were lacking in science, technology, and the new learning. The new breed was clever, resourceful, and energetic; they were also vigorous, aggressive, arrogant, and unstoppable. Many came from Protestant Northern Europe, burning with a mission to trade, conquer, and teach. Conquest and trade, however, would precede any teaching or altruistic endeavors—for example, roads, trains, hospitals, and schools.

Thomas Roe and his many colleagues and rivals opened the gates of exotic Asia. They opened the doors to future alliances and aggressive trade and to a new era for India and, indeed, the rest of the planet: Western learning, trade, exploration and, in time, domination. Eager to embark on the quest for new Asian riches, the East India Company grew into a powerful enterprise with ships, captains, soldiers, sailors, and guns—and deep capital. They were guided and funded by an ambitious London-based board of directors. They surpassed—with more guns—all their rivals and became the first major multinational company in the world. They had ships, bustling docks, and warehouses in London and many other ports. They were sending flotillas of ships to the shores of India and beyond—including Burma, China, and Indonesia. They pushed aside the Portuguese, who were not so adept at colonization. The British were pragmatic, less bigoted, and driven by a sense of almost messianic fervor. They were going to conquer and make money, but they were also going to improve the lives of the natives. Yes, they were going to improve the world. These, after all, were the Protestants who saw man, not just the Church, as an instrument of God for change and social development.

The mighty East India Company, backed by London wealth, guns, and soldiers, moved into the vast new territory with vigor, facing a divided and confused India now that the Mughals were waning. They established new and powerful trading posts, forts, and towns around the shores of India: Surat, Bombay, Calcutta, Madras, and many others. Soon they were expanding beyond the ports; they were land grabbing. Nobody said that in one hundred years, we are going to have a British Indian Empire: it happened step by step: little wars, acquisitions, treaties, broken treaties, another battle, more land, more treaties—and a growing sense of power and confidence, as well as immense wealth. They gobbled up the lands of local rulers and princes and introduced an efficient and European style of taxation. They introduced roads, postal systems, trains—armies and merchants must move fast—forts and more soldiers. In the ports—besides the intimidating rows of cannon—there were huge warehouses of goods and many ships coming in and out of the harbors.

The British were more cunning than the Portuguese, Spanish, or Dutch: They trained loyal natives to serve in their armies, borrowing this strategy from the French. These natives, called sepoys, were led by elite British officers, many of them on horse. The horse was the mighty engine of war, fast and big and frightening. No one in Asia had confronted an English cavalry charge of several hundred well-trained men armed with swords, lances, and revolvers. Not only were these men skilled in killing; they were highly trained, efficient, and loyal. In battle they were brutally effective—and terrifying to foot soldiers—and they hardly ever backed down, no matter the odds. Furthermore, the Europeans were improving the methods and means of killing, not only with new guns but "scientific" tactics—now taught in their military academies—using artillery, cavalry, and foot soldiers.

Incredibly, the British would control most of India, supplanting the increasingly weak Moghuls. The British were a tiny minority, but they used a successful combination of aggression, bribes, threats, cunning, treaties, and appeasement. Local maharajas would be allowed to keep their own little fiefdoms—but for a price! The Mughal rulers became less effective and more degenerate—opium and women—more intolerant and narrow-minded. The Taliban mentality set in. Those of intolerant views and cruel actions never establish flourishing societies, and in time Mughal emperors were weak and ineffective.

By the time the British captured Lahore (around 1850), they defeated not an army of Mughal warriors but an army of Sikhs who had set up a small, vigorous kingdom in that part of the Punjab. British India became a reality—indeed a fabulous reality—and emerged around 1850 as the biggest and richest colony—the jewel in the crown.

The British Indian army unwittingly encountered a serious payback. When they captured Lahore and the Punjab, they had a new northwestern border. Their empire now touched the lands of the Northwest Frontier, bristling with fierce, hostile warriors, and the formidable headache, Afghanistan. And overnight, a new bogeyman emerged: On the other side of Afghanistan, the Russian bear was lurking. This notorious Northwest Frontier became the wild west of the British Empire, brimming with stories, battles, and excitement. Tales of evil and valor emerged from the Frontier, and the British reading public were enchanted.

British fears were not all paranoia. Russia did have its eyes on Afghanistan—and India, the precious jewel—and they made some scary moves: spies, secret battalions, and cunning treaties. The British became obsessed with controlling Afghanistan and policing the unstable Northwest Frontier. The Russian and British rivalry in the region, called the Great Game, involved dangerous cat—and—mouse games. It lasted for one hundred years! As an aside, it is very strange that as I write America and Russia are deeply embroiled in a simmering — and potentially dangerous — contest in the Middle East.

It is tragic that after all those years of foreplay, the Russians eventually did invade and control Afghanistan in 1980 with disastrous results. Somehow, the Western nations did not get it: You always lose when you try to control Afghanistan. On the planet, there are few tribal warriors as fierce as the Afghanis and the Pathans, their neighbors in the Northwest Frontier. They had hundreds of years of hard training. Afghanistan, a particularly rugged country, is a precarious crossroads in Asia. The locals are—to this day—only too familiar with foreign invaders. Strangely enough, it was because of these tribal hotheads that my ancestors came to that part of India. Because of them, the British army encouraged my grandfather to develop Renala, a horse breeding farm for the border patrols and the feared cavalry.

The cavalry needed a certain kind of horse that was not commonly found in India at that time: a tall, strong, dependable, trainable horse, one that could carry his officer into a raging battle, or up a steep mountain pass, or along a narrow trail through rocks and desert. This horse must be able to ride many miles and work closely with other horses. The cavalryman, in particular the border patrols, were the rugged special forces of the day. They could travel fast over rough terrain, hit hard, and disappear.

Their foe, the Afghanis and Pathans, were wily mountain men who knew every nook and cranny and were brutal in war. To the young British soldier, this rough region guaranteed action and thrills. Around these rugged men—both English and Pathan—legends and stories grew, and for many they became the giants of the empire, something tangible to believe in, something dashing to look up to, or someone to fear and hate. All the young boys of England and other countries would read their stories and flock to the movies. Often, they were accompanied by their sisters and parents!

SIX

GO EAST

For over three centuries, thousands of Europeans were enchanted by the lure of the East. There was adventure and opportunity and escape from farms and factories and poverty. There was hope in a time when there was little social movement or chance for advancement. They would go as farmers, traders, soldiers, and civil servants. Sometimes they had little but the clothes they carried. There were no lending banks, unless you were rich; there were no scholarships, travel-abroad programs, or easy solutions.

As the empire in India grew, more were called to join the long, dangerous passage east. And once in India, there was no going back for holidays or if your mother was sick. If your mother was dying in London, the letter would arrive after she had passed away. Many jumped at the chance to go east, despite the dangers and, for those days, incredible distances. A journey east could take several weeks or more and was fraught with dangers: typhoons, pirates, foreign ships, and disease. Tropical diseases brought down countless hale and hearty lads from Liverpool and London. But the lure of the East was powerful and would not slow for another 200 years.

The first Vanrenen arrived from South Africa in about 1781. I have a letter from a great, great uncle explaining the coming to India of a young South African, Jacob Vanrenen. South Africa, located strategically at the tip of Africa, is where the tough Dutch settlers had first arrived in the sixteenth century as traders on their way to Eastern markets, and pilgrims escaping Catholic persecution. They were soon followed by English settlers, especially after gold and diamonds were discovered.

Jacob's grandfather, Jacobus, had emigrated from Prussia in around 1740, escaping—as the rumor goes—from the law, as he had killed a man in an illegal duel. Young Jacob, living in South Africa, is orphaned, and adopted by a friendly English captain; he travels with him to England but, tragically, his adopted father dies. Jacob returns to South Africa as a young man. This chapter of his life introduced the Vanrenens to England and changed the spelling of their name. Without any prospects in South Africa, he does what many young men of his time did: he shipped out to India on one of the many trading vessels of the East India Company. He was on his own, heading off to a completely different world.

He left no letters, as far as I know, about his feelings as he boarded a cramped ship, *The Osterly*, bound for Calcutta, India. He must have felt lonely and scared, but like any young lad, he quickly made friends with some of his fellow passengers and sailors, some of whom were in similar straits. It was a long, rough passage to India, fraught with high winds, pirates, typhoons, and doldrums. In his satchel he carried a letter from the clerk of the shipping company: a promise of employment when he reached Calcutta, as a cadet in the East India Company. On board for those weeks, he busied himself with deck work and chores, and the comradery softened the reality of a strange destination with no certain end. Little did Jacob know, but this precarious journey was the start of an exciting and long career as a soldier in India. Jacob's history is not lost, as he and his offspring would be included in a book, a fascinating document. In 1924 Joubert De la Ferte, a distant relative, would publish a book, *A Notable Record*. The subtitle of this book: *Some account of the many families descended in the Male and Female lines from Daniel Van Renen {and first wife*

Catherine Chritiana {Beck}, second son of Graf Jacobus Von Rheneen or Van Renen, who as soldiers, Sailor and Airmen served Great Britain. It was from this book that I would gain an overview of the Vanrenen presence in India and other parts of the great empire: Africa, Australia, and the Far East. The book includes numerous genealogies, but for my interest, the genealogy of Captain John Henning Vanrenen of the British Indian cavalry is most pertinent. He was born April 4, 1804 and died January 4, 1867. The son of Jacob, the first pioneer, John Henning would marry Yda Johnna (DeNys) of South Africa, and they would have nine children, one of whom is my great grandfather, Jacob Peter Denys.

All these people, going back to 1781, would serve in India and most of them as officers in the esteemed cavalry, the heart of British power. Some, special forces of the day, would die in obscure battles or skirmishes in lonely and hostile Afghanistan, the Punjab, the jungle of Burma, or the deserts of Baluchistan; some would be shipped overseas to fight in the Anglo–Zulu War in South Africa, or some other dangerous region on the other side of the map. They were a proud bunch, judging from their photos, always very much part of their "elite male club," the cavalry officers, a significant cog in the massive engine of empire making.

The British in India all shared a rock-hard value: a belief in their mission and purpose. Even if their main intention was job and money, they were still moved by their mission: the good that they could do—or thought they could do. From an early age, they were indoctrinated in the beliefs of their country, religion, and empire. They and it were all one. What they did, even if horrible, was for Queen, God, and country. Conquering some obscure tribe somewhere in India had some intrinsic value! This is true with people of any empire in any period of history, including America. How long did it take us to admit our wrongs toward Indians and African Americans? We did the same thing in Vietnam, and we embarked on a disastrous empire war in Iraq, and on and on. And yet America, with its principles of good governance enshrined in the Constitution, is a unique and powerful nation.

I see these Vanrenen pictures and names, a whole chain of people going back five generations. What were they like as human beings? It is hard to generalize, of course, but the men were like any professional soldier serving under a mighty power. They were part of a tight club. This provided security in mind, body, and heart. They could be generous and kind, at times, especially to those of their type, but they looked down on signs of "weakness" or uncertainty. There were no big questions to ask, no great religious fervor, and no need to go beyond the rule. They were often hale and hearty in athletic recreation and in relaxation, prone to drink and gruff talk and laughter. They were rarely non-conformists. They followed with a dogged persistence and had little patience for "other" people, colored, gay, or just plain different. They often scorned artists and art, and they were contemptuous of those who walked their own walk. They showed little interest in the Indian culture or religion. They showed affection and patience for their women, at least much of the time, but women were second tier, which was common in many cultures of that time. They were marked by the values of their country and time: often patriotism, bigotry, zealous mission, high energy—and all the related values of any people who live and breathe empire. In their work they were zealous and professional, rarely deviating into corrupt self-interest—which made their system a workable and efficient machine. We have seen this type in America.

Jacob, the original Vanrenen in India, arrived as a lowly soldier, but—as was the dream for many—he rose in the ranks and became a successful and respected officer. At a certain point, an officer of distinction would, as they said, raise his own regiment, hire and train Indian soldiers to march, ride, and die. The British were a tiny minority in a huge country and they could never have conquered and ruled alone. Jacob raised a regiment of loyal Indians who followed him into many battles across the breadth of India. Jacob persisted, a tiny cog in the grinding engine of empire building. He would marry and raise a family of nine children and serve with distinction for fifty years without any extended furlough. This was one tough guy! He would retire with honors, his full rank a brigadier general, and die at

This is the only image of Jacob I could find, from a miniature painting. At this point, he is a highly respected general in the British Indian army, and father to nine children, many of whom would raise large families, and all of whom became British Indians, the men serving in the cavalry. In time, one of these would be my father, Walter.

a ripe old age on a boat near Cawnpore on the Ganges.

Sadly, I know so little about this man. I do know that one of his sons was the father of my great-grandfather. Of my great-grandfather I know little but possess two marvelous photographs, which will be displayed in this book. He was also an officer, a colonel in the Fifth cavalry, a legendary regiment in the British Indian army.

Denys Henry, my grandfather, was born in India, the fifth son of Jacob Peter Vanrenen. Like most Anglo boys of the time, he was sent back to England for schooling—a long and lonely time—and then attended military college and went back to India for posting. This strange upbringing must have hardened many a young lad, whose mothers became strangers. Denys was then posted to the Remount Unit, which raised and trained horses, an important function in the era before cars, jeeps, and trucks.

Important for the family, at an officer's dance in Lahore, he met a beautiful young lady whose parents had a tea estate in faraway Assam. Her name was Ysobel Butler, a woman with a royal bearing, befitting her German ancestors. She was dressed in a lovely blue and white gown, with thick curls of auburn hair, and a charming smile. The rugged cavalry officer, tall, rigid, and handsome, with his ornate uniform and cap, became awkward in her startling presence. Ysobel, more relaxed and humorous, soon put him at ease. They would complement each other well, and, in time, enjoy their life at Renala. Both did not shy away from hard work, but also shared a love of horses, family, and friends. They were British Indians to the core, and shared all the values and pride of their "tribe."

Denys Henry, posted near the Northwest Frontier, was asked to pioneer a horse-breeding estate in the region. They needed healthy dependable horses for the Indian cavalry and for those dangerous border patrols. He and his cohorts searched the empty scrub jungle south of Lahore, and they chose an area that could be serviced by British canals. The seed for Renala was born. Hard work—much of it done by Indian laborers—ensued: forests cut down, fields created, roads, houses, and a fine central building for the family. There would, in time, be neighboring Indian villages to house the workers for the farms, barns, and fields. This was a hugely consuming project, accomplished in a region serviced by a train that connected to Lahore.

Renala was born in 1913, just before World War I. It flourished from the start, and even more so when DV—grandfather was often called DV—retired from the army to breed champion race horses. In 1914, Renala Khurd, the neighboring town with a railway stop—from Lahore—was born, and today is a growing city.

SEVEN

WALLY AND ZIZZA, THE NEWLYWEDS ARRIVE IN INDIA

Wally was born in Lahore at the English hospital, just like his father, two sisters, and my sister, Cal. When my mother first met Wally, he was a handsome young lieutenant in the Central India Horse, a regiment with a long pedigree. I once asked my mother how one got into a regiment like that. It was, like so much else in social life, through connections. One had to be introduced to the right people, who would then vet you, and others would vouch for you, like an elite country club. Once "in," you acquired prestige; you had pay, title, and uniform, but you had better toe the line or life would get very unpleasant. And you had better have some extra cash to pay for the horse and its upkeep. Allegiances were tight, obligations were fast, and duty never wavered.

Zizza knew that once they were married she would leave her family and country for a long time. But she didn't mind. She was bowled over by this terrifically handsome officer in the British Indian Cavalry. She looked forward to her new life in India. She had an adventurous streak. She was not a little flower girl who nodded her head. Many of her friends were jealous. It was the thing to do. It was exciting. Everyone in England, even in the little villages, had been exposed to the "romance" of India!

After the long journey through the Mediterranean, they landed in the great port city of Bombay. Disembarking was always a thrill: palm trees along the shore, the silhouette of an Asian city, and the great bustling docks with mobs of strange people in varying attire. The air had strange aromas, some floral, and it was humid and hot. Porters with blue caps would greet the tired passengers and offer their services. The well-off British traveled with mounds of boxes and trunks that were then loaded onto carts pulled by skinny little brown men in bare feet. For Wally, this was old stuff. But he was excited about returning to India and Renala, proud of his beautiful wife that he would soon introduce to his friends, colleagues, and family.

For Zizza it was all a thrill, but also a little frightening: a strange new world with noises, aromas, and sights she had never seen. From the docks the rickshaw man, followed by the cart of trunks, would take them to the old grand British colonial hotel, the famous and ornate Taj Mahal, with the dressed-up servants, the hoity-toity staff, and the cavernous vestibule. They would stay a night or two before the train ride north to Lahore, and the much-anticipated arrival at the grand estate of Renala where they would be greeted by the staff and the family.

Well, that must have been a moment for Zizza. Their car honked its horn as they drove through the grand gates and up the curving driveway to the elegant colonial mansion, staff and family waiting in front smiling and waving. As Zizza got out, Wally's mother, Ysobel, stepped forward and shook her hand, smiling and welcoming, and turning, she introduced her to the staff as if they were family. Zizza would never forget that first encounter, the calm smiling face, the erect but relaxed posture, and the steady eyes. Sadly, Wally's father was not there to greet her. He had recently passed away, buried near Cannes in Southern France. She would never meet the legendary and formidable DV.

And in a few days Wally would be back on the job, posted to another military barrack, what the British called cantonments. The officers always brought their wives along, unless there was an emergency or war. Zizza and Wally would travel to a series of cantonments in the Punjab and beyond, beginning Zizza's amazing adventure in the waning British Indian Empire. She would be there for almost ten years.

She would experience the colonial grandeur of Renala with its shining black horses, dignified staff, servants, and regal garden; she would witness fabulous races and polo matches in grand stadiums around India; she would travel to Lahore and dine at the cavalry officers clubs—members only; she would witness with thousands the march of the Viceroy of India, followed by the cavalry in their finest uniform, one hundred dressed elephants in tow; she would travel to the great Himalayas and lodge with Ysobel in her mountain retreat, the view of snow-capped peaks from her window; she would see working elephants, trained cobras, Indians of all classes and professions; she would make friends with Indians; she would have fun and adventure with Wally: trips to the Maharaja's palace, the tiger jungle, and races in Lahore, with cocktails at the officers' club. She would get to know the other officers in their circle, the handsome and curt, the jolly and humorous, and, of course, she would socialize with the wives, gossiping, drinking tea, and plotting. She would make friends with Wally's mother, Ysobel, who was now a widow, and during the long years of World War II, the two of them, with Zizza's baby daughter, would spend good times together.

My sister Val was born in a hill town—with the unlikely name of Ootycamund—in Southern India, and sister Cal was born far north in Lahore. Zizza would learn to cook—or at least help the cook; she would tentatively manage the servants, and, of course, help take care of the babies. She would learn to navigate the intricate social intercourse with the fellow officers at the clubs and races. She would learn the challenges of being a young mother and wife in a strange and foreign land. At first it was strange for her, unaccustomed to these manners and lifestyle, but, in her heart, she was a democrat and friend to all, not a ruling person! She would remain so her whole life, quite different from those in her husband's circles.

The most thrilling time was the visits into the Himalayan mountains, to the little resort village of Gulmarg, a little England with golf courses, cottages, tennis, and the club where they ate, danced, and drank, and, of course, the flowery gardens that the English loved. Another segment of her life involved extended visits to Renala where she became close with Wally's mother, Ysobel, the matriarch of the estate.

All this time, a terrible storm was brewing in Europe. Germany, it would seem, collectively swallowed a strange pill and became a psychotic nation following a loud-mouthed Austrian private and former street artist named Adolph. Germany was now a dangerous nation; Germans were now number one in industry, technology, and war machines. They would, amazingly enough, be led by a charismatic speaker who, with his inner circle, were experimenting with cocaine and amphetamines—a fact I did not learn in college.

In 1939, World War II began, and Zizza became a war widow in Renala with her young daughter and Ysobel. And as if to make the situation especially odd and perilous, the same disease afflicted Japan. The ferocious Japanese Empire started their march toward India— much to the shock of the British high command, who had no idea that Asians could match the British in technology, war machines, and battle.

The proud Raj now had several mortal enemies, much like one of those medieval tales of the heroine circled by roving monsters and devils. But most significantly, India now had an energetic independence movement, one that picked up steam during the war. The unthinkable was about to transpire.

Wally and Zizza, looking very slender, on a brief holiday in Kashmir, Northern India, right before Wally was posted to the war in North Africa. Their precious time together was coming to fast and dramatic conclusion: It would be five years before their lives were restored. They stand below the ancient ruin of a tower. India was dotted with magnificent relics from its storied past. Some say that the first great civilization emerged in India before Egypt and the Middle East.

EIGHT

LIFE IN INDIA FOR THE BRITISH

Rudyard Kipling, the great writer of the Raj, was a marvelous talent who produced poems, stories, and books, including the much-loved *Jungle Tales*; *Kim* (the novel); and *The Just So* stories. But many modern critics find him offensive because he was a staunch imperialist, a promoter of the Great British Empire—and in particular, British India. Offensive or not, he was a prodigious writer with fine instincts. T.S. Eliot called him one of the best writers of verse in the history of literature.

Kipling would spend a good portion of his early adulthood in Lahore, a city that played a key role in my family, as it was the major city near Renala. About the time Kipling was a young lad, my great-grandfather was an officer in the Bengal Lancers. At the same time, they might have both visited the Lahore officers club to enjoy a beer or drink a gin and tonic.

Kipling lived in Lahore in a simpler time: there were no phones, trucks, or cars. Kipling's father, a museum curator and artist, worked in Lahore, and like so many British Indian parents, sent his son back to Britain for schooling—a lonely time that Kipling would write about. Imagine being a six-year-old boy, sent off on a ship to England to live for some years in a tiny boy's school run by an eccentric headmaster.

On holidays, he would not see his parents, but stay with fussy elderly Victorian aunts. No wonder he became an avid reader and writer.

After schooling, Kipling returned to Lahore where he became a journalist for a Lahore paper that published six days a week. He wrote local stories, traveled much, and got to know the lives of the Indians and the British. He visited the British barracks and threw down a few beers in the mess. He was attracted to the manly ethos of those rugged men, but he also walked the Indian streets and saw how the "other" side lived, and how the common British soldier worked out his dreams.

A fabulous image of the old market section of Lahore over one hundred years ago. This was a magical street to walk down, and even to this day in Asia, some of the cities have remnants of the old market streets.

Wally was also sent back to school and would not see his parents for several years—the only transportation was a slow ocean voyage. This separation deeply influenced the lives of those young men who made their careers in India. They did not have many memories of a cozy decade growing up with mum and dad. They were often soldiers, drinkers, loners, and driven to succeed.

The ambitious Kipling would leave India saturated with Indian stories, sights, and ambience. He would become the grand old writer—consorting with royalty—of the British Empire. Kipling, in fact, lived during the final years of Queen Victoria, at a time when Britain peaked as a world power and excelled in science, world exploration, literature, and many other fields.

Queen Victoria, who never visited India, was considered by many, including Indians, the grand Mother of India, and her statues, buildings, and image could be found all over the country at that time. She once said that she loved her Indian subjects, and there is no doubt that she took her role seriously.

Wally and many of his family spent the greater part of their lives in India. When one lived in India, there was no flying home to see Granny for a week. One went back to Britain on extended leave for a good reason. Even Wally's full-blooded British Indian family considered England home and kept a house in Kent, but they rarely had time to visit. What of homesickness? Home, in those days, was really far, far away—like the moon. In one poem, called "Christmas in India," Kipling wrote:

> The dim dawn behind the tamarisks—the sky is saffron-yellow—As the women in the village grind the corn, and the parrots seek the riverside, each calling to his fellow
> That the day, the staring Eastern day is born.
> O the white dust on the highway! O the stenches in the byway!
> O the clammy fog that hovers over earth!
> At home they are making merry 'neath the white and scarlet berry –
> What part have India's exiles in their mirth?

The British in India were often lonely tea planters in the hills soldiers stationed at some hot dusty barrack in the middle of nowhere— surrounded by a sullen and strange people; or if privileged civil servants, they might live in palatial homes in the leafy suburbs of a great city, but they were always strangers. India was hot and huge. India had a teeming population of all kinds of people and castes who wore odd clothing and lived lives far from what the British considered the norm.

But many made the most of it and even loved it. I think my grandparents, Ysobel and DV, loved it, but only to a point. It could never be home.

A rare photo I received in 2018 from Peter Vanrenen, who runs a sheep farm in Australia, of our great grandfather. Jacob and his lovely wife, Francis. A colonel in the British Indian Army, he married Francis in 1873. She is dressed in the Victorian attire, not so comfortable in the hot Indian climate. He is dressed in some quixotic oriental clothing, a real charming fellow. One of Jacob's sons would be my grandfather, another, Peter Poleman Vanrenen, who would move to Australia. In a nice synchronicity, I received a message from his grandson in Australia, also Peter, just before sending this book to the publishers; also, some unique letters and photographs, a few that have been used in this book. I discovered that we have a large and vigorous branch of our family in Australia!

In India, the British tried their best to recreate the look and atmosphere of home: They loved to retreat to little cottages in the cool hills, in villages with gardens, a recreational club, and a stone Anglican church. Not particularly devout, the British in India were largely of the Church of England. On Sundays they would sometimes go to the local church where there was an English vicar reading from the Bible and singing hymns. The British Indians often favored what is called "muscular" Christianity with rousing hymns often with a nationalistic flavor, such as "Onward Christian soldiers marching onto war, with the cross of Jesus going on before." Many of the British soldiers were, at best, nominal Christians. Their "church" was often the mess hall or club where they ate, drank, and socialized. There was much drinking: Gin, whiskey, and brandies were favored, as well as beer. Chai, or tea, was common, and because fresh milk was rare, the British doused their tea with canned milk and sugar. In their off hours, when they weren't drinking, they would be off riding, boxing, hunting, or, if privileged, playing polo.

Energetic and hard-working, the British built roads, railroads, government buildings, forts, tea and coffee plantations, museums, schools, towns, and cities. Much of the labor was, of course, Indian. To India they brought a system of transportation, a nationwide legal system, and schools and colleges—teaching, of course, the modern curriculum. But for a "real" education—and this would include privileged Indians—England was the place.

In the church or club, the British could fraternize as if they were back home. They were snobs and would rarely allow any Indians (except, of course, the staff) into the club. One exception, however, was the elite Indian aristocrats who often outdid the British! There was lots of drinking, whiskey and gin being the drinks of choice; there was also gossip and flirting. Affairs even afflicted the prudish British. No humans can put the lid on the power of sexuality, and the British in India were simmering with suppressed sensuality. This, by the way, was in a country with very attractive men and women, Indians who dressed in charming and colorful dress. My mother once confided to me that Indian men are gorgeous and the Indian women, they turned many an Anglo-Saxon head. What a strange stew it all was!

The British, accustomed to the cool climate of England, often struggled in the Indian heat. Besides the tropical climate, plants, and strange animals, they were living amidst a teeming population of diverse people, from tribal desert people to sophisticated city dwellers to primitive people still living in jungles, and an amazing array of languages, religions, and races. The British had to also contend with an army of insects—mosquitos being number one. Malaria, a nasty virus carried by mosquitos, afflicted people living in the tropics. Contracting malaria could be a serious business, with recovery taking months or longer. It was a British doctor in India who first scientifically equated malaria with a virus transmitted by mosquito. Quinine from a tree bark made a good antidote, and for this reason British in India drank quinine drinks round the clock.

The greatest horror, however, was the poisonous snakes, and India had its share. The most feared snake was the king cobra, of which Kipling would write his famous story: "Rikki Tikki Tavi." Horrible and strange diseases took many British to an early grave: diseases of hygiene like cholera and also strange tropical diseases, leavened by an occasional plague. All this sounds positively awful, but people did thrive in India. Like the locals, the British regulars became adaptable and hardy and learned the skills of survival and good living in a tropical climate.

Imagine being a little English child in India. What a strange and sometimes terrifying journey, but also magical with the Indian nanny—so kind and faithful—the peacocks and monkeys, the journeys to the cool and clean mountains, and the host of sights including all those Indians! The English child, lonely in a foreign land, would make friends with Indians, either children or adults working in the household.

The British had little choice but to get used to the heat and humidity of India. In the very hot summers, those British who could escape work did: They went into the cool, green hills of the Himalayan

Adrian Vanrenen with his Ayah, or Indian nanny, circa 1880. Every little British child had their faithful and loving Ayah, someone they might remember with fondness in their elder years when retired to a little English cottage in Dorset. This remarkable image came to me recently from my relative in Australia, Peter Vanrenen. I was astounded to see that Peter's family in Australia is large and thriving, and that they have been there for well over a hundred years.

Mountains. Ysobel and her family went to the lovely hill town of Gulmarg where there was a hotel, cottages, and homes, as well as the requisite golf course. The British Indian government leaders retired to Simla for the hot summer months. In fact, for six months of the year Simla became the "capital" of India. My mother told me that the poor soldiers or planters who were forced to stay in the hot plains (up to 110°) were often miserable: alcoholism and even suicide were not uncommon.

During World War II, Zizza and Ysobel spent some good times in Gulmarg, which helped them to get to know each other well. Of course, it was not all fun and games as the threat of imperialistic Japan and Nazi Germany was real and quite alarming. Many of the Indian soldiers were fighting overseas for the empire, in Europe, North Africa, and Burma. And some Indian regiments, like the Gurkas (mountain people from Nepal), were known for their skill and valor. If no one else could do it, send in the little Gurka warriors who never shied away from the impossible.

The British in India had little interest in the rich spiritual tradition of India that literally soaked the country like water. Many considered the Indians heathen and looked down on their religion, but to their credit they did not repress Indian spirituality. Even if the average British Indian was not an avid Christian, there were enough Christian fanatics—those who felt that Christian white people had a mission to save the world. Kipling displayed this viewpoint in his notorious "White Man's Burden," a poem that glorified this mission. Indian religion and spirituality is like a diverse forest from the devout wisdom of leaders like Gandhi (whose favorite book was the Baghavagita, a world masterpiece), to fake gurus, to holy men of gentle presence, to the chants and songs of the country folk, and, also, a deep contemplative philosophy of living well. India has a rich and ancient history, which includes many sacred texts, many cults and religions, dance, yoga, poetry and music, and beautiful temples.

Perhaps the spirituality of India had a subliminal effect on some of the British, who would then go "home" with Indian lore and wisdom. Today in England and America, yoga, an import from India, is as common as sports; meditation—where India had a tradition going back thousands of years—is now discussed at colleges; and many ancient Indian texts have been translated into English. Mindfulness, a state of awareness practiced in India for centuries, is now on the cover of *Time* magazine and discussed at Harvard Medical School.

Despite their snobbery, the British in India were impressed by the diversity and grandeur of India: the magnificent scenery, the animals and birds, the astonishing temples, the architecture, the songs, the bright clothing, jewelry, craft, the range of people and customs, the rich literature, and the nobility of the Indian himself. The British would retain their sense of superiority—one of the foundations of any empire—but could not help but be moved by the many faces of Mother India. Many of the British had Indian friends; they knew the local language, or enough to get by; and they developed a taste for Indian cuisine. India had a food culture that was tasty, diverse, and sophisticated. The British—who came from a country with a notoriously dull cuisine—developed a taste for curries, samosas, rice pudding, ginger beer, and tandoori chicken. Every English family of distinction had an Indian cook who had to learn—poor person—the way of English cuisine but also display her or his native talent on the dining room table. In fact, the "native cuisine" soon replaced the stale fare imported in boxes and cans.

The British in the army, like my father, developed a quaint way of speaking: Anglo-Indian English, often an English with an occasional Indian word or expression. I grew up with a little of this, as my father had spent a majority of his life in the shadow of great India. Some of the British in India became fluent in an Indian language; they would visit a menshi, a language teacher, who might become their first Indian friend. India, by the way, is a world of many languages and dialects, like a huge bubbling stew, which is one reason the English language became common, and still is!

My cousin Jean, who spent some time in the family home at Renala, would hear my grandmother speaking Urdu to the staff. And she remembers bedtime in the grand old colonial home, upstairs in the soft bed with the mosquito netting. Ysobel, or Granny Van as she was called, would come to Jean's bedside and sing Urdu bedtime songs. Jean regrets that she does not remember the words. I happened to find a version of this Urdu nursery rhyme:

Talli,talli badja babe	*Clap, clap hands baby*
Ucha roti schat banaya	*They make good bread*
	In the market
Tora mummy kido	*Give some to your*
	Mummy
Tora daddy kido	*What is left over*
Jo or baki bai ayah	*Give some to your old*
Burya ayah kido	*Ayah*

Years later, a tough former soldier or memsahib back in England in retirement would remember these words and sing them to their grandchildren. I heard bits of songs, sayings, and poetry from my mother. In her era, people were not addicted to the Internet (of course, it did not exist) and often had time to memorize poetry and songs and to tell stories—one of the great gifts of humanity. How many people today can recite a Blake poem or the Psalms or some nursery rhyme? It is an extraordinary but simple gift.

It is a curious fact—and a testament to the influence of British India—that American English has adopted more than a few words that the British bought back from India. A bungalow is a Bengali word for a little cottage or house. A thug is a nasty bad guy. Thuggis were an Indian cult of murderers and robbers whom the British eradicated. Bandana, bangle, chintz, chit, chutney, dungaree, cushy, loot, musk, pariah, punch (the drink), shawl, khaki, pajamas, yoga, pundit, and veranda are other words that permeated American English, but there are many others.

British India has been gone for a little over 70 years, but many Americans know hardly anything about it. True, there have been BBC movies that revive the topic from time, but British India is largely an embarrassment to many Indians, a dim memory to the English, and barely a blip in the consciousness of Americans. So many chapters in history! The one we are in now will someday soon be lost. In the following pages, we can taste an era that, for those living it, seemed like a fabulous adventure that would go on forever.

Kipling captured the images, excitement, and wonder of life in India. In him, the British Indians found a voice that spoke to their imaginations and hearts. But he also, like all great poets, touched the hearts of many people of any age or culture. One of his great triumphs was the children's book *Jungle Tales*, which Kipling wrote in snowy Brattleboro, Vermont. The snow was high outside the windows, the fire warm, and when he sat down at his desk in the lone, quiet Vermont far from India, this idea for a story came to him: He had heard an Indian tale, one that went back centuries, of a little boy who grew up in the jungle and became friends with the animals. Before he knew it, his pen took off across the pages—as he himself said. In time, his story would enter comics, movies, games, and he would become famous.

When I was a boy I would read, as most British children did, Kipling stories. "Rikki Tikki Tavi" is a delightful tale about a brave mongoose—a fierce weasel-like animal—that saved the British children from the dreaded cobra that had crept into a bungalow. The mongoose not only could match the cobra; they also reveled in the joy of mortal combat.

The lure of the East captivated many, including many in my father's family, and an air of it is found in the well-known verse *Mandalay*, which Kipling wrote while in cold Britain. In this and other verse, he sings of the romance, dreams, atmosphere, and exotic sights and people of lands far from Britain. It is a long poem; I will only quote the first section. Kipling is best read out loud.

By the old Moulmein Pagoda, lookin' eastward to the sea
There's a Burma girl a-settin', and I know she thinks o' me
For the wind is in the palm trees, and the temple-bells they say
'Come you back, you British soldier, come you back to Mandalay!'
Come you back to Mandalay
Where the old flotilla lay:
Can's you 'ear the paddles chukin' from Rangoon to Mandalay?
On the road to Mandalay
Where the flyin'-fishes play
An' dawn comes up like thunder outer China
'crost the Bay!

NINE

THE NORTHWEST FRONTIER AND ITS IMPORTANCE FOR THE FAMILY

North of Renala, the family estate, was the rugged and formidable Northwest Frontier, the wild west of British India. Inhabited by independent and warlike people, often called Pathans, it consisted of valleys and mountains. Each valley could have a different tribe, sometimes not friendly to the neighbors. These fierce people—the men always carried a dagger and rifle—considered the British an alien invader, and for over one hundred years the British attempted to manage these mountain people. It was a hundred year war.

This ominous photo by Uncle Louis depicts a British fort in the dangerous Northwest Frontier. Forbidding and isolated, it reminds one of a fort in the old American West. Life was hard in these frontier forts, as they were always susceptible to attack; water and supplies could be scarce. Camel caravans would bring in supplies, ammunition, and food. The camels were managed by a man called a sowar, an expert in camel behavior (camels can be stubborn and mean). Sometimes the camel caravans were attacked and robbed and all the men and camels killed, so the fort would be stranded for months with dwindling supplies. The Pathans, local tribesmen, were skilled at stalking, robbing, and killing, and had little fear. They loved to steal guns, and every Pathan had a 20-inch blade tucked into his belt.

A stunning antique photo from my Uncle Louis' collection. Notice that there is no leading British officer. This, I believe, is a Sikh regiment that fought for the British. The Sikhs, respected for their courage and skill, were a dominant society in the Punjab. We see a little boy in front. What an unusual education for a boy: He was a bhisti boy, the water carrier, water being a major need in Indian warfare.

A British artillery regiment in action during the third Afghan war in 1919—from Uncle Louis' collection. The British made great use of artillery during the India days, and often the guns were pulled by mules or even elephants. The artillery men were well-trained, acting in frightening tandem with brutal effectiveness. Opponents often had little or no artillery.

In 2001 the planet was captivated by images of mountains of Tora Bora on the edge of Afghanistan and the notorious Northwest Frontier. Osama bin Laden and his band of rebels, on the run from American forces, escaped into caves of that almost impenetrable region. Bin Laden, of course, had engineered one of the most infamous acts of terrorism in world history. No one who witnessed it on television will ever forget the image of the collapse of the Twin Towers, the proud icon of Western capitalism. Bin Laden, tragically, knew exactly where to hit.

This wily man, a scion of a rich Saudi family, would then disappear. What ensued was one of the greatest manhunts in world history, involving thousands of soldiers, agents, and computers in America and around the world. Despite his infamy, bin Laden had apparently disappeared, but in 2010 his image once again captivated the world. Doggedly tracking his associates, American spies finally found his hiding place, not a cave hideout in the Afghan mountains—as most supposed—but a comfortable house in a settled region of Pakistan.

In one of the most exciting news items of the decade, American Navy Seals raided his home at night with helicopters on May 2, 2011;

they landed and penetrated his home in a daring raid. They found and killed the most notorious terrorist, a dramatic raid that would spawn numerous articles, books, and movies. At the time of his death, bin Laden was not hiding out in some remote mountain cave, but in a large, comfortable house in Abbottabad in the Northwest Frontier, not far from a Pakistani military outpost. The irony of the name, Abbottabad, escaped the world, but this town was named after a famous British cavalry officer who operated in the Northwest Frontier—now part of Pakistan—in the late nineteenth century. General Sir James Abbott not only gave his name to the town; he founded it.

In his early career James Abbott rode and fought for the British Indian government in the highlands of the Northwest Frontier. Legendary for his skill and courage, he often led wild bands of tribal warriors—fiercely loyal to him—and once was known to force the surrender of a whole Sikh army using a small band of Yusufzau irregulars. He and his cohorts would strive to do what many had attempted for years, even centuries: tame the Northwest Frontier, a thorn in the side of proud British India. There was no taming of these people. It is ironic that one hundred years later, America is playing the same game in Afghanistan.

James Abbott would leave Abbottabad in a very different manner from Osama bin Laden. Bin Laden, who pictured himself a hero for the downtrodden people of Islamic nations, was deluded by his anger and prejudice. He believed in a world-wide jihad to destroy the enemies of Islam and create a world Islamic state. He neglected one of Mohammed's greatest teachings: the jihad was the holy war within: with our own divisions in heart and mind. He lived and died a troubled man whose legacy of 911 would stain his name forever. There are some Islamists (the dualists and extremists) who still consider him a hero. Likewise, there are people who still revere Hitler. Bin Laden was a rigid dualist who saw the world as good and evil, white and black, us and them, me and the world. The sense of liberating oneness never permeated his rigid consciousness. From Saudi Arabia, he was raised in the Wahhabi sect of Islam, notorious for their intolerance. Unlike most Muslims, one tenet of Wahhabism is to kill the infidel, not only Christian but anyone who is not one of them, which, strangely enough, could include other Muslims. This is, of course, contrary to the heart of Islam and Mohammed.

James Abbott, made frontier deputy commissioner in 1852, was known for his valor, honesty, and kindness. Contrary to the picture of the cruel Brit colonialist, he favored the local people and Indians in general. He was known for his kindness and generosity, and when he entered a village, the people would come out to greet him, including the children. When removed from his administrative position, it is said he used his own money to throw a party for his constituency, a three-day bash. He loved to wear fine Indian uniform with a turban, and indeed in the London National Portrait gallery one can find a portrait of this unusual man wearing a colorful turban. What is especially touching is that Mr. Abbott, upon leaving Abbottabad, wrote a poem:

I remember the day when I first came here
And smelt the Abbottabad air
The trees and ground covered with snow gave us indeed a brilliant show
To me the place seemed like a dream. And far ran a lonesome stream
The wind hissed as if welcoming us. The pine swayed creating a lot of fuss
And the tiny cuckoo sang it away A song very melodious and gay.
I adored the place from first sight And was happy that coming here was right
And eight good years passed very soon And we leave you perhaps on a sunny noon
Oh Abbottabad we are leaving you now To your natural beauty do I bow
Perhaps your winds sound will never reach my ear. My gift for you is a few sad tears.
I bid you farewell with a heavy heart. Never from my mind will your memories thwart.

Bin Laden would depart from Abbottabad in a completely different way, gunned down in the late night horror show. Colonel James Abbott, however, left peacefully. One can see him riding out of town on his horse, looking back one last time.

Abbottabad, in the Northwest Frontier, is close to Renala. My uncles passed through here, as did other members of the family. Uncle John, nicknamed Jumbo, was for a short time a member of the famous Guides, a Frontier cavalry, consisting of mostly local troops.

It is this rugged region that had such an influence on the life of my family. And even Zizza, the young lady from Kent, would explore the region, and make the "pilgrimage" to the entrance of the Khyber Pass. Zizza, in fact, engaged in some unusual adventures during her India years.

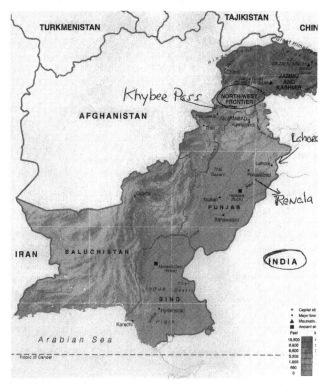

The map shows the modern country of Pakistan, with Renala, Lahore, and the Khyber Pass marked. One obvious geographical fact is that Pakistan is wedged between India and Afghanistan.

A British military expedition heading off into the rugged mountains in search of an elusive enemy. The mountains make the regiment look like miniatures, and indeed they were. Lurking behind every rock, or on top of any cliff, could be a Pathan sharp shooter. Even with primitive rifles they were dangerous, but when they managed to steal or buy a modern British rifle, they became lethal. They would kill a few British soldiers, cause havoc in the troops and horses, then disappear into the hills like phantoms.

Military camp, Northwest Frontier, with horses, horses, horses, the all-important horse. The cavalry was a crucial part of the army in these rough tribal mountains, and it is conceivable that some of these horses came from Grandfather's farm. In this photograph, they are being led out to relax and feed. Keeping the horses healthy and strong was a big challenge: they needed regular food and lots of water and were always susceptible to injury.

This is a typical fort in the rugged Frontier. You can see how desolate, dry, and hot it could be. These lonely outposts were sometimes exposed to terrifying attacks by local hotheads who would swoop down at night, firing rifles, screaming, and playing drums. Furthermore, the Pathans had great skill in firing a rifle: They were said to be some of the most lethal marksmen the British ever encountered. Uncle Louis obviously came through this fort—since he took the photograph— which looks like a fort in the old American West.

The tribal people of the Northwest Frontier are a complex patchwork of different tribes, but they all share one common feeling: a distrust of foreigners. These hardy people are also cursed by a code of revenge known as the blood code—where a man is forced by tradition to right any wrong committed against him or his tribe. In the British days Pathan warriors would lie in wait behind rocks for hours, through snow and rain, waiting for a chance to pounce on an unsuspecting soldier or trader. They would sometimes crawl naked, so not to create a rustle, in the dark of night, carrying only a knife in their teeth.

John Masterson, the British writer, was stationed in the violent Waziristan, and witnessed the most terrifying conduct in war: European wounded would be tortured, castrated, and left to die. The British always made a desperate attempt to collect their dead, as even the dead bodies were exposed to indignity. But these mountain people have many sides and were often admired by the British for their valor and generosity. When you gain their trust, they are firm friends.

While many Pathans are Muslim, they have a preference in the end for their own traditions. However, they have a long history of being swayed into war by extremist Muslims. They have an ancient traditional form of governance, based on jirgas or tribal councils. These councils make all important political decisions and also act as judges. There was no one leader or king, a system that was puzzling to the British.

The Northwest Frontier was the wild west of the British Empire and many fables, adventures, and tragedies emerged in the rough region peopled by proud and rugged tribesmen. Many movies were made, even Hollywood movies. Books were written, as well as comic books, poems, and paintings. As late as 1959, the British made a rousing action film with Lauren Bacall called *The Northwest Frontier*.

There is a famous British Indian painting by Lady Butler; it is a desolate image of a man, barely hanging onto his horse, as he approaches the safety of a fort. It depicts the final chapter of Britain's disastrous 1841—1842 invasion of Afghanistan. The story is told by only one man, a British medical doctor, who escaped the terror of

Gunga Din, one of many Hollywood movies, released in the 1930s about action in the Frontier, where British soldiers put down another uprising by the vicious "savages." The title is from a Kipling story. Cary Grant and Douglas Fairbanks, debonair and heroic, ride into the wild Frontier to quell some "native" troubles: as the ad went, "Out of the glory of Kipling's India..." The honorable white sahib—on his horse!—would capture or kill the dark-faced villain and his mob of fanatics. It was the Wild West in India, right down to the fierce savages and noble heroes. Occasionally, a good guy could be Indian, but he always played a subordinate role: loyal, dependable, even funny.

massacre in the infamous Khyber Pass. The British Empire leaders were incensed by this terrible loss—especially since the Afghan king had promised safe passage—and sent back an army of retribution that outdid the cruelties of the Pathan warriors.

In the Northwest Frontier, many British soldiers lost their lives, but the frontier lured many and captured the imagination of the British public. And despite the dangers, some went there for adventure and to make a name for themselves. Winston Churchill, as a young officer and journalist, visited the region and witnessed the perilous battle of Malakand, a conflict between British and tribal forces. The ambitious 23-year-old aristocrat, eager to make his name, sent back reports to London newspapers, and eventually published his first successful book: *The Malakand Field Force,* which depicted British heroics against fierce, unkempt, tribal savages.

The British did win the terrifying battle at Malakand, where a small British force was attacked by a host of tribal warriors who had been incensed by some rabid Mullahs. Sound familiar? And one cannot completely discount the Mullahs' warnings: The British were a strange occupying force that now controlled the whole Northwest Frontier of India. Pathan tribals were a complex bunch: they were not adverse—for a fee—to fight for the British against their brothers. But they could be quite capricious, and at the turn of the coin, join the other side.

My father's family, for several generations, were posted in this rough area, and both my grandfather and great-uncle fought in the infamous third Afghani war. Our relatives rode and fought in countless engagements over one hundred years. Some, I am sure, were buried in unmarked graves in the wilds of Afghanistan. The British occupation of the Northwest Frontier turned into a hundred-year war, with hostilities, sorties, and battles never ending, no matter what the well-equipped British army did in retribution. They had fine cavalry, Indian regiments, modern weapons, and mountain cannons. They even employed elephants to haul artillery up mountain valleys. It reminds one of the so-called war against ISIS. When and if ISIS disappears, another head will emerge, no matter the phenomenal power and technological skill of Western armies. People fighting for their rights, land, and dignity have remarkable resilience and courage.

For the British soldier to be stationed in this strange and wild world was an adventure, to say the least. Some hungered for a posting there. Here is an anecdote about a young British soldier posted to the Frontier, introduced to the ways of this strange world. The regiments were often a mix of races, even in the officer class, and in the wild world of the Frontier, everything was different. The following excerpt is an amusing picture of one British soldier's experience.

We walked over to a tumbledown hut, which was the Adjutants'
office. A group of big, bearded men sat there on the bench. They
wore voluminous white robes and held walking sticks between
their knees. Another group, without walking sticks, squatted. The
squatters were bought to attention by the NCO. The squatters
arose, saluted the adjutant, and looked at me sternly. I was
introduced and shook hands with Rissaldar Major Mohamed
Amin Khan, Jamadar Harrrat Gul, Rissaldar Sultan Khan …
names that made my head reel.

They all said Salam Hazoor (to which I answered Salaam
Sahib) except one Indian officer, who disconcerted me by saying
'Janab Ali,' which I afterwards discovered meant 'Exalted
Threshhold of Serenity,' or more literally, 'High Doorstep'.

In the course of these introductions [Ressaldar] Hamzullah
[Khan] arrived. We shook hands. He eyed me narrowly, cackled
with laughter and made a remark to the adjutant in Pushtu, the
language of the frontier. The Adjutant translated.

"He wants to know if you can ride. He says you are the right
build. And he says you are a pei-makhe halak—a milk faced boy."

I was anything but pleased.

(quoted from *Bengal Lancer*, p. 290, by F. Yeats-Brown)

My grandfather Denys Henry was an officer in a unit called Remount, which was very important in those days. Remount bought horses (sometimes from overseas) or bred dependable horses, then trained them for the cavalry. One doesn't just hop onto a good horse and shout "Charge!" The horses needed to know the ropes, take commands, and be comfortable in all situations. Denys Henry, an adept horse man, had mastered the art and science of breeding horses. Horses were extraordinarily common in those days, prior to the truck or jeep, and, quite obviously, the foundation of the cavalry. A man going into battle on a horse would want to know that his animal could be trusted completely. Battles were chaotic and noisy, really a terrible situation for all involved, and you didn't want your horse to panic.

In the days before the car, a good horse was not only a necessity, but a good friend. The horse would often have a special name and treatment, just like some people nowadays treat their cars. I will present an anecdote about the friendship between a cavalryman and his horse.

I have allowed him to take shelter in my tent and in return, he lends me his rug to sleep on. The tent being small there is not much room to spare, but he is the most discreet of horses, never thinks of turning or kicking his legs at night, and so we sleep side by side, as comfortable as possible...He is as good as a watch dog, allowing no one to enter the tent without my leave and always wakes me in the morning by pushing me with his nose the moment he hears the bugle sound.

(quote from Lieutenant Campbell-Brander, *Sword and Pen*, p.71)

My grandfather, and his immediate ancestors, and for some time my father, were a part of this strange world—the world where horse was king.

This photo shows the beauty of the mountains of the North. One can see why members of my family, and soldiers like James Abbott, fell in love with the area. This photograph is painted by Ysobel, who lived before the era of color photography.

TEN

COLONEL HOLDICH AND THE NORTHWEST FRONTIER

For over one hundred years, members of my family were involved in "the shenanigans" in the Northwest Frontier. But one made a name for himself in the history books, particularly in the field of geography. In 1886 Ada Vanrenen—sister to my great-grandfather—married the esteemed Sir Thomas Hungerford Holdich. Unfortunately, I know little about Ada, but her husband became a well-known man. He, and a team, were in charge of establishing Indian borders, most dramatically the border between Afghanistan and India. Colonel Holdich, head of the commission to establish this critical border, did much of the work—with a team that included Indians—on foot and horse through rugged, often hostile mountains.

Thomas Holdich, circa 1890, and his beautiful wife, Ada Vanrenen. These two photos came to me unexpectedly from my cousin in Australia, Peter Vanrenen, who is the grandson of my great-uncle. I had lost hope of finding a picture of Ada Vanrenen, but not only did he send me eight photographs of her, but also, amazingly enough, a number of her letters. She would live a happy life in India and England.

Holdich would write a wonderful book about his Afghanistan expedition called *The Borders of India*. It is a fascinating account of his life as the chief officer of the Afghan boundary commission. Officer, cavalryman, surveyor, political agent, and savvy leader fluent in several local languages, the colonel was a remarkable man. Furthermore, he was well versed in Pathan dialects and knowledgeable about their traditions and ways. In his time off from surveying, he would live with his wife, Ada, and socialize with the Vanrenens, including my great-grandfather, at the officers' clubs. But Ada was, more or less, a widow as her soldier husband preferred surveying expeditions that took him away for months.

Upon his retirement, Colonel Holdich and Ada returned to England and for two years he was the head of the esteemed Royal Geographic Society. When he died, his obituary in the Geographical

Journal praised him as the most knowledgeable man about the borders, people, and tribes of Afghanistan and the Northwest Frontier. This is a stunning accolade considering that this is one of the most rugged and dangerous regions of the planet—that he accomplished what he did and lived. There were times when he had to have the stamina of a young mountaineer, the skills of multilingual diplomat, and the courage of a mountain lion. On foot and horse, he and his team trudged for months through often hostile territory to survey and establish the scientific borders of the Northwest Frontier. His demeanor commanded respect, and even hostile chiefs would acknowledge his presence.

Colonel Holdich was an empire man to his bones, a true British officer, but he was observant about people and nature and kind in his dealings with Asians. His fair dealing, courage, knowledge of languages, and sense of diplomacy kept him from assassination, quite common in those lands. He was also a skilled painter, a passion he shared with my grandmother, Ysobel, and my mother, and painted the mountain scenery. A down-to-earth man, he never sought grandeur or fame, and would retire after twenty five years of rugged experience on those perilous borderlands. His retirement, however, consisted of more work as the head of The Royal Geographical Society for two years, and other ventures, including a grueling challenge to settle a serious border dispute between Chile and Argentina. He and his wife, Ada, had two sons, both who would, of course, join the British Indian army.

Below is a charming story told by the colonel on one of his many surveying trips into the borderlands.

Between the wood-smoke and the tanning effects of the wind and weather, many of the door-rugs acquire a tone which is not matched by any other artificial process, and we took them eagerly whenever we could persuade the fierce, wrinkled old Turkman woman to part with them. First advances were usually made through the rosy-cheeked, cheery little Turkman children. A present of a few beads would produce ecstasies of pleasure;

but it wasn't until the children were allowed to retain the beads by their parents. I remember one little damsel of six or eight whose delight was expressed in every line of her sweet little form when she first took the strong of blue beads from my hand. Then she showed the beads to her wizened fierce old grandmother, who was watching the proceedings with fierce but bleary eyes from the darkness of the kibitka interior. I don't know what passed between these two, but the young lady returned with an expression of infantile dignity that stiffened her little limbs, and curled her lips into the funniest affectation of disdain that ever was seen and would have done justice to an actress. So far it was exceedingly well done, but she waited just a little too long. A childish look of longing stole into her eye: and it stayed there, and disturbed the theatrical pose of her head, and then a large, unbidden tear appeared. I did not wait to see any more, and I do not know what became of the beads.

(page 120, *Indian Borderlands*)

Below is a photograph by Uncle Louis of four young tribal girls, one of whom could have been the young lady in the story above!

A fascinating historical photograph of a treaty being signed on, I believe, the Northwest Frontier. The central figure could have been Colonel Holdich, but it is some other chief officer. In front, a group of British officers sitting at a table; in back stand the "native" militia. This photograph from Uncle Louis' collection has an unknown origin, the date circa 1870.

This photo from my uncle shows the bare hills of the Northwest Frontier, with a fort, and an army in front, ready to be deployed. Colonel Holdich and other relatives witnessed events like this many times. The border line, which he helped create, was and is still controversial because, for one, the Pathans have yet to accept it! To the Pathans, and all the people of the frontier, the creation of this border was travesty, even worse.

The photo depicts a high mountain valley with an expeditionary tent and grazing sheep.

A delightful photo of a tribal woman who is about to get married. In the background is the laughing husband, finding it humorous that the Englishman, Uncle Louis, wants a picture of his bride!

In one beautiful paragraph, Holdich describes looking out from a mountain top over the serene views of smoky valleys. He realizes that he is probably the first European to stand on that mountain—in a vast sea of mountains—and perhaps the last. In the valleys below, however, life was not so serene, and every month he encountered scenes of violence and extremism.

Today, if we think that "terrorism" and religious extremism are new, we are gravely mistaken. Holdich and other British encountered this phenomenon each year, every year. British presence and actions only fueled the fire and made the locals more prone to listen to the "mad" mullahs. The Pathans thought the British invaders were from another planet. What strange men in their fancy uniforms and hats, their odd talk and mannerisms, and their arrogant behavior! Likewise, the Pathans had their strange behaviors and traditions, but they, at least, were living in their own world.

A dignified old gent from the Frontier region wears his bullet belt; he is rugged, tough—someone not to trifle with—but also hospitable and kind. The Pathans lived in another world, far removed from modern Western ideas, science, democracy, and book learning. Women were second-class citizens, but that was true of all India including the English. Uncle Louis—who took the photo—knew this man, whose name I do not know.

The following excerpt from Colonel Holdich's writing describes another battle, but notable is the emphasis on the cavalry in this engagement. The Mohmands was one tribe particularly known for their cruelty and violence. As their name implies, they had been converted to Islam, but unlike other tribes, they did not have much good that could be said of them. Also, note that this particular "uprising" was inspired by a fire-breathing Mullah.

> *Rumours had been afloat that the Mohmands contemplated rising for some days previous to the actual outbreak …and it was not till Shabkadar (a fortified post eighteen miles north of Peshawar) was attacked, and the old Sikh town … burnt, that a movement was made to check the outburst. The glare of the burning village could be seen from Peshawar on the 7th of August, and that evening a small force marched out to disperse the enemy. On the 8th occurred that memorable fight that was especially distinguished for the gallant charge of 13th Bengal lancers. Through and through the over-confident hosts of Mohmands did they charge. It is not often that the hill-men are caught in the open by cavalry. They were caught then … this was one the most brilliant cavalry charges in recent British military records. It settled matters for the time, and allowed breathing space for the formation of a punitive Mohmand field force, which then swept through the land. The Hada mullah was for the time discredited.*
>
> (from *Borders of India*)

His phrase, for the time, is very telling: It was like putting out a forest fire, every time one is extinguished, another rises up nearby: When the new Islamic nation of Pakistan inherited the Frontier from the British, they improved relations with the mountain people by letting them police their own lands. The British had tried this sensible policy in a small way. But even with modern transportation and communication, the Frontier is still a region of unrest and ferment for extremists. The Taliban, while not indigenous to the Frontier, have infiltrated and stirred up confusion, as always. The continuous news of perpetual "troubles"—extremism and war—has not changed one tiny bit; today, however, these are now global. Acts of violence rock London, Madrid, and many other cities and towns around the planet, and not just remote mountain villages in the Northwest Frontier.

ELEVEN

NOTABLE PEOPLE ON THE NORTHWEST FRONTIER

Many famous people lived in or visited the Northwest Frontier. Some were Indians like Gandhi, who would visit during his liberation struggle. On the other side of the coin was Winston Churchill, who visited as a young officer. Churchill, notably, made his first foray into fame because of his journalism work in the region. There were many others, but for me, the following three are particularly interesting.

FRANCIS YOUNGHUSBAND

A British man who had a deep attachment to India was Francis Younghusband. Younghusband, a most unusual British Indian, was born in 1873 in Muree, India, his father a tea planter. Murree is a pretty mountain resort about two hours north of Lahore and Renala. For those British residing in the Punjab or Northwest Frontier, it was a favored retreat in the hot summer months; cool fresh mountain air, a quaint little village, and lovely views in all directions. Most important, it was peaceful. On Sundays, the ladies in white would stroll with their parasols down the main street, then enjoy teatime, and perhaps some golf or tennis in the afternoon, and dinner at the club in their finest.

In his time, Younghusband was a famous explorer, writer, and philosopher. In his early years he would live the life of a typical British Indian lad headed for the military. Like my father, he attended a top "colonial" training school, Clifton College in England, separated from his father and mother for years, then graduated from Sandhurst, the military college my father attended. And, like my father, he would return to India a British Indian officer but would head off in his own distinct direction. An adventurous man, he made a challenging, to say the least, trek from China through the Gobi Desert, over the Himalayan Mountains and into India—something few, if any, Europeans had done. Other exploits included helping to organize the famous "Mallory" expedition to Mt Everest, the highest mountain on the planet.

Younghusband was also involved in a controversial exploit: He would lead a British military expedition into the heart of Tibet, the capital Lhasa. No European country had accomplished this prodigious feat. Traveling through rough high-mountain terrain, the plucky British beat up a tiny army of ill-defended Tibetan monks and marched into the Tibetan capital with the Union Jack flying. For the Tibetans, and perhaps the planet, it was an ignominious and propitious moment. For the British, this fiasco was a result of their great game with Russia, and their hubris—both of which caused much distress to Tibetans, Indians, and others. Younghusband, the leader, would come to a bad feeling about his role in the "Tibetan adventure."

In the remote and magical Lhasa, the capital of Tibet at 15,000 feet, Younghusband, uncharacteristic for any British officer, felt the tug of a new emotion. He conversed with learned monks, was given a tiny statue of the Buddha—which he would treasure his whole life—and before departing for India, mission accomplished—he hiked to the top of a mountain where he, unexpectedly, experienced a revelation: a mystical opening into the wonder of nature and life. One can only conclude that the sustained duress of the dirty little war and his own deeply sensitive nature conspired to open his heart to its most subliminal knowledge.

"What came upon me was far more than elation or exhilaration ... I was beside myself with an intensity of joy, such as even the joy of first love can give only a faint foreshadowing of. And with this indescribable joy came the revelation of the essential goodness of the world. I was convinced past any refutation that men were good at heart, that evil in them was superficial ...in short, that men at heart were divine."

(The above quote is sited in Patrick French's excellent book, *Younghusband*, Flamingo, 1995, p. 252)

This profound experience—for the steely British Indian officer—would change his life. He would, in time, forgo his military career and India to return to England to promote the unity of all people and religions. He would continue, for some time, his career in British Service, including serving for two years as president of the Royal Geographical Society, at the time the most esteemed institute of its kind. He would take this post right after my great uncle, Sir Thomas Holdich, vacated this position.

Younghusband, inspired by his spiritual insights, would veer off in what many considered bizarre eccentricity, promoting ideas that are now current: the world mother, our planet, mystic unity, meditation, yoga, and tolerance and respect for all people and religions. He would write books about mountain exploration and mystical religion and begin various organizations to promote peace and unity. And, amazing for the old colonial imperialist, he would display respect for Indian spirituality. He even spoke highly of the spiritual value of sex between man and woman, at a time when this was a forbidden subject. Of course, many of the old school shook their wooly heads, but Younghusband was ahead of his time, and ours. With his wife, he retired to a little village in Kent, not far from where my mother lived as a girl. Retire, however, is not the right world, as he remained vigorous in many activities, teaching, lecturing, and networking with his soul mates—those who shared his deep vision for transformation of self and society. He would be blessed by a relationship with a lovely woman, not his dour wife. Younghusband, his big moustache now white, would pass away, a healthy and happy old man, during World War II.

When he was a young officer in India, British India was very much alive; he rode horses with his saber and pistol, part of a generation that saw the last of the cavalry charge. There were no cars, trucks, phones, highways, malls, e-mail, or radio during his early professional life. He would pass away when Hitler—another rabid dualist—was threatening world peace with gas chambers, bombs, trucks, tanks, rockets, radar, and planes. But Francis would not die with regret or despair—no, in his optimistic heart, good would triumph. He lived and died well.

ABDULAH KHAN, BADSHAH KHAN, THE FRONTIER GANDHI

I don't know if Younghusband ever crossed paths with Gandhi's comrade, Abdulah Khan, but he did meet Gandhi, whom he admired. Mahatma Ghandi, who for over 25 years led the Indian independence movement, is one of the most famous people of India. The task of gaining independence was of such great difficulty and duration that it is incredible that one man could accomplish what he did. Gandhi, however, had many allies and helpers, men and women, and one in particular I would like to mention.

Abdulah Khan, a close colleague of Gandhi, was a highly unusual man. For one, he also had the title Badshah Khan, which meant king of kings. He was from the Northwest Frontier—not so far from Renala—and a Pathan, the rugged tribes famous for their courage and violence, especially when their code of honor was broken. One other fact about this Khan, whose family were landowners for generations, is that he was Muslim. Gandhi, as we know, was a Hindu whose favorite book was the sacred scripture *Bhagavad Gita*. In this modern era of extremism and rigid mental habits, we might be surprised that Muslim and Hindu not only became allies in the quest for independence; they became close friends. And both men suffered immensely in their quest for independence, including repeated times in prison. They literally gave their lives, twenty four hours a day, to this quest.

It is interesting to note that Badshah Khan had been influenced by English thought at an early age: He would attend a British Frontier school where he was exposed to the kindness and learning of a Mr. Gordon. Perhaps the best fusion is a meeting of Eastern spirituality with Western learning. He would never forget this missionary teacher, but he would go off into a spiritual trajectory that was distinctly Asian.

To many, it was odd that a rugged Pathan would become an advocate for peace, tolerance, and non-violence. This tall, noble man reflected the benevolent side of Islam, a quality often knocked aside by the belligerent extremists, who, of course, are not true followers of Mohammed. The reactionaries of any religion or political faction are always dualists; they live in "the two," me and them, I and the world. This projected division is a reflection of their inner division. Islam, and its mystic side of Sufis, is a religion that advocates compassion and kindness to all. It is not inherently reactionary or violent. At its roots, it is founded on the inner journey toward unity and wisdom, the true jihad that Mohammed spoke about.

Badshah Khan and Gandhi were united by common aims and values. They both knew that the holy war, the jihad, was the inner war with our own deep divisions, angers, reactions, and fears. Today, and in the past, some of the fanatics are compelled to avoid the inner struggle and project their frustrations out into the world, manifesting as violence and anger. Badshah Khan exemplified the tremendous effort that is needed to rise above the inner divisions we all share. He was truly a giant of his time.

Gandhi was short and thin, a small man with a big spirit. At 6 feet 8 inches, Badshah Khan towered over his friend; they looked like the odd couple. He promoted a Gandhi movement in the Northwest Frontier, stirring up what the British considered "troubles." He would be arrested and imprisoned for weeks, but the British could not help but grudgingly admire the gentle giant. His "army" of peaceful Pathans numbered in the thousands, a great achievement for that or any time.

Like Gandhi, he advocated for a unified India, not an India divided between Hindu and Muslim. This more inclusive view was not popular with either the Islamists or the nationalist Hindus. He would speak in public, educate, and advocate for his own people, the often-disregarded hill people of the Northwest Frontier. He never deviated from his life of peace even when he was cruelly mistreated. Change, political and personal, could only come from peaceful intentions, based on an understanding that, deep down, we are all alike and share the same need to be a part of something real and integrated. We are not all little isolated islands. The prison of dualism, me and the outside, us and them, cannot be let go of easily—most of us remain dominated by this little ego.

Of course, my grandfather Denys Henry had heard of Badshah Khan in the 1920's. On hearing his name, the British would raise their eyebrows or mutter curses. He was, as they liked to say, a "troublemaker." Denys Henry was on the other side of the fence, but also a man of strong values. He was a part of the military presence in 1919 that would restrict the wildfire of Indian strikes—it is even conceivable that he met Badshah Khan. That year was a turning point for India, for the Punjab, and the Northwest Frontier. It was the year that General Reginald Dyer ordered the massacre of over 300 Indians in what he considered an illegal demonstration in Agra, not more than an hour from Renala. That tragedy rocketed around the world and created tremors in the independence movement and India. It must have shaken the confidence of those at Renala.

My grandfather, a part of the military presence at the time, was commended by the British authorities, but deep down he and many of the other British ruling class sensed the tremor of coming changes. The truth of all empires is that the ruling class is blind to the need for change. In America, we have seen this repeatedly: for example, the Vietnam War or the disastrous war on Iraq.

The year 1919 was also pivotal for Renala and my grandfather, hence the coming generations. My grandfather would retire—perhaps eagerly— from the army, retreat to his booming business in race horses, and ride out his last years as a successful CEO of Renala. He would, and I know nothing about this, flirt with writing and journalism for a few years. I do know that he had suffered a broken hip from a fall from a horse, and this accident sent his body on a downward course. All around him radical change was in the air, and all the British, following World War I, were sensing this undercurrent.

Badshah Khan and Younghusband shared a similar vision, not only in their heads, but in their hearts. Not so strange that a Pathan and an Englishman from the Northwest Frontier would come to a place in the heart that denied the divisions, rivalry, and violence that have afflicted the human race for thousands of years. In the end, Younghusband respected Indian spirituality and independence, much to the dismay of his colleagues. He remained, however, a staunch fan of England and English culture. He had become, one could say, a true universalist, not just in words but in his mind and heart. In these two men, so different in looks and background, we see the hope of mankind, not in ideologies, defensive postures, nationalism, or religious "right," but in a common vision, hidden deep in their feelings. Younghusband's vision and feeling are similar to my mother's in her later years.

Badshah Khan spent most of his adult life advocating for his people and independence. He got into repeated trouble with the British, in and out of prisons, but when independence finally happened, you might think that his life would become "like roses." On the contrary: He jousted with the new Pakistani government. His special wish was to create an independent country for his people, the Pathans. The Northwest Frontier would become Pathanustan. But this would never happen. The Northwest Frontier was incorporated into the modern Muslim nation of Pakistan, which inherited the headaches of the British. The indomitable Badshah Khan would live to a ripe old age of ninety six, never abandoning his principles of peace and non-violence. Today, as mark of our times, both Gandhi and the Khan are not as valued as they should be, even in India. The inner work of self-refinement is, perhaps, too great a hurdle for people today.

FAKIR OF IPI

This rabble-rouser and "terrorist" was opposite Badshah Khan. As a boy I heard this odd name from my mother and never forgot it. The Fakir, the bin Laden of his day, was a shadowy fellow, very slippery, who created multiple headaches for the British, particularly in the Northwest Frontier. In the 1920s and 1930s, "the mad Mullah" drummed up opposition to British presence. Outposts were attacked at night, convoys ambushed, fiery speeches delivered at mosques, and mysterious assassinations occurred. All this sounds very familiar.

All the British knew his name, and many despicable things were said about him as he hopped around like a ghost fanning flames and rousing the tribal people. No doubt over dinner at Renala, there was a lot of headshaking and name calling. They just could not catch him, and unlike bin Laden, he evaded capture and died of sickness in 1960! Over the centuries there have been many men like the Fakir, but he eluded capture and lived to an old age.

There was another reason that my mother knew his name. During the war, Zizza worked for military intelligence in Lahore as a code decipherer keeping watch over the Northwest Frontier and Afghanistan. The Fakir of Ipi was high on the radar. Strangely enough, Zizza's sisters worked in a similar capacity, but in London and Bletchley, the famous code-breaking center north of London. Sarah, her younger sister, continued this work after the war and traveled with Lord Mountbatten on his Asian missions. I regret, as in so many other instances, that I did not encourage Zizza to tell me more about her experiences as a "codebreaker."

In the military intelligence building at Lahore, there was another name my mother heard: the Wali of Swat. Swat is a mountainous region on the northern edge of the Frontier, and the Wali was the lord of the area. This particular Wali was a suspected Nazi sympathizer. His "sympathy" for the Nazis circled around his hope that the Germans would send him precious modern rifles. The British were worried that the Nazis would influence the Afghanis to ferment troubles in India.

So for a time, the Fakir, the Wali, and many others tormented the

British during their tenure in the Frontier. The Fakir, however, was a genius in guerilla warfare and a clever opportunist who pocketed funds and weapons from Russia and Germany, but in the end, he did not care for global Muslim causes, Russian advances, or Indian independence. He wanted liberation for his territory. Like bin Laden, he would hide out in cave systems and vanish in a flash, and he had active support from locals. They considered him a warrior and holy man, and he would gain a reputation for creating miracles. It is certainly astonishing how he evaded British intelligence for all his life. It was uncanny, too, how his "double," Osama bin Laden, would return at the end of the twentieth century, only this time the bad news would resound around the planet—not just British India—for years.

In this dramatic arena—of so many warriors and "bad guys"— there were and are many good men and women. For example, one of the spiritual fathers of modern Pakistan, Muhammed Iqbal, lived in Lahore. He would have been there at the same time as my grandfather, but it was doubtful that they met. This remarkable man, a lawyer trained in London, would become a celebrated writer, very different from the Fakir of Ipi. Iqbal, a cultured man, conversed with many people including the British. He would become a mystic poet of great stature, writing in Persian, Urdu, and English; he would die in 1938, seven years before the birth of his beloved vision: an Islamic state for the Muslim of India. Today, his birthday is a national holiday in Pakistan. A Sufi, he expressed many fine sentiments and ideas, a most dignified man to instigate the difficult birth of Pakistan.

Upon the death of his beloved mother, Iqbal wrote a short poem that anyone who has lost a mother can identify with:

"Who would wait for me anxiously in my native place?
Who would display restlessness if my letter fails to arrive?
I will visit thy grave with this complaint:
Who will now think of me in midnight prayers?
All thy life thy served me with great devotion—
When I became fit to serve thee, thou hast departed.

LAWRENCE OF ARABIA

Another celebrity who passed through the Frontier was none other than Lawrence of Arabia. Lawrence's presence in British India is a curious story, and few know that he was briefly stationed in a British outpost in Waziristan, one of the most dangerous provinces of the frontier. In the beginning of his illustrious career, Lawrence was a young officer in colonial Egypt prior to World War I. Having traveled the region and become familiar with the languages of the Middle East, he became involved, somewhat by accident, in the liberation of the Arab people from the Ottoman Empire. He would adopt his role as a friend of the Arabs with gusto. With this feat, he became world famous, and the photo of him wearing Arab dress would rocket around the planet.

After the war, Lawrence became disappointed when the British and French divided up the Middle East and turned back on their agreements with Lawrence and the Arabs. Disgusted, Lawrence would enlist in the air force, change his name, and retreat into anonymity. He wanted to be known as Airman Shaw, a regular guy on the job. He mostly did clerical work, posted to the middle of nowhere in the Sind Province, India, south of the Punjab. His barracks were in the middle of the desert, and there was nothing for him to do but his work, writing, and correspondence. Airman Shaw was not pestered too much by his fellows—they, of course, knew who he really was. Word naturally got out that he was posted in India, in fact in the Sind not far from Lahore where my grandfather worked. Denys Henry had retired from the army and turned his attention to race horses. On the side, he did some journalism. Hearing the news that Lawrence was just down the road, so to speak, he wrote an article in the Lahore paper asking Lawrence why he was hiding out. He also favorably reviewed Lawrence's recent book about his days in the desert with the Arabs. Lawrence, incredibly enough, replied to my grandfather, using a antique typewriter and lots of corrections! The letter has never been published. For almost 90 years, it has hidden in a wooden box that holds family papers, and one day, many years ago, my father gave me a copy. It is a curious letter because of its messiness—he was perhaps impatient because he did not really want to reply—but it is 100% Lawrence. Below, I reproduce two pages of this curious correspondence of Lawrence to my grandfather.

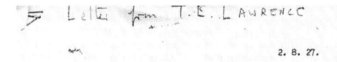

2. 8. 27.

Dear Looker-on,

Your expectation that I might read your article was just. Two of our fellows brought it to me today, and begged me to answer it. I explained that writers never replied publicly to reviews, and that to write privately was dangerous, lest the other man gives me away. They contend that it's a decent article, and yourself patently all right! So here goes, for once. Please consider it aimed at your personal eye, only, and do not attempt to make the public wise. Be more discreet than myself.

I can't agree that I'm "Concealed in India". The district knows that I'm at Drigh Road. The newspapers do not publish it, for the editors suspect that their more foolish readers might bother me; and if my presence in his camp becomes troublesome to a C.O. he tends to take it out of me. Since 1923 there has been no secret (in the R.A.F. any way) as to my service, name, rank or whereabouts.

Also please don't insult the R.A.F. by talking of its "soldiers". That's the final term of abuse, between airmen. Soldiers are to us Sergeant-Majorish persons, lovers of clicked heels and jerks. Soldiers are team-servers, effective according to their obliteration of themselves as parts of the machine. Airmen are masters or servants of machines, and are efficient in proportion to the individual intelligence each can put into his particular job. And it's some job , this combined attack on a new element. The ideals of air and army are as far apart, and as commonly confused, as socialism and anarchy.

The passage you quote from "Revolt" dates, like the rest of the book, from the winter of 1919-1920, and it was written in London, years before I enlisted. The later revision, in barracks, xxxxxxxxxxx affected only details of style. But it is true that I had been in the ranks, before the war; and from 1919 my intention had been to enlist, as soon as I was free to do so.

You make something of my "assumed" name. "Lawrence" was assumed also. Shaw is as legally my name as a deed-poll can make it. You know that English law regards surnames only as a convenience: and Lawrence became, to me, a very convenient label.

I apologize for beginning every sentence with "I". ————⟶

105

ᶜ ¶ I wanted the Arabs to have xxxx leave to make their own mess: and not
to go on holding their hands to save them from messes. Peoples learn
by falling down, like babies,.

This letter gets too long. It's as long as your article, and not
so good. More apologies. But if you ask a man to explain his life he
can't, unless he is a Balfour, put it on a half sheet of notepaper.
I'M in the R.A.F. because I like it and when people offer me larger boots,
and talk of my wasting my "talents" (save the mark) in the ranks, I comfort myself
with the sure knowledge that there's nothing else my talented self wants to do.

Perhaps I should explain that I'm broke, financially, because I think
my leadership of the Arab Revolt was a fraudulent proceeding: and I'd
be more ashamed of myself than I am, ₤ if I profited by it. You may say
that the fraud succeeded, and that those who speculated with me received
their reward. I think they got more, in proportion to their desert, than
any other of the allies: and it is an "nglish custom to promote the successful
promoter to the House of Lords. But to mk my judgement success is perhaps
the blackest sid e of a swindle.

This letter must stop. If ever you pass through Karachi between
now and March 1930, and feel energetic, do drive out the six miles to Drigh
Road (I never leave camp bounds) and assure yourself that I'm an average
specimen of quite contented humanity. There is no mystery and no romance —
after you have seen me in working clothes!

Yours sincerely,

338171 AC II Shaw
    Room ERS,
        R.A.F.
            Drigh Road.

At the end of the letter, Lawrence says: "This letter must stop. If ever you ever pass
through Karachi...there is no mystery and no romance—after you have seen me in
working clothes!" Lawrence had had his fill of attention and just wanted peace and
quiet. This, however, was not the end of Lawrence's tale in India or his international
publicity. His superiors, nervous about his presence in India—on "Drigh" Road in
the middle of nowhere—got edgy and word got out. The press in London howled. The
authorities packed him off to the Northwest Frontier, to a dangerous and inhospitable
region called Waziristan.

This Waziristan was an odd choice for a posting, one of the most lawless and perilous regions and closely aligned with defiant Afghanistan. Stationed in a lonely mountain base, his presence, once again, began to make big-wigs nervous. No doubt, some were a little jealous that this man with the title of private was more famous than any of them would ever be. Furthermore, there were rumors circulating that Lawrence was acting as a spy, that he had been seen in a Pathan outfit, possibly with the intention of sneaking around in Afghanistan. Lawrence of Arabia now would be Lawrence of Afghanistan, creating trouble in the Wild West of British India. This unfounded—that is the consensus—rumor from a London paper ignited another firestorm of publicity for poor Lawrence.

To the public and press this sounded thrilling. London politicians demanded an explanation, and in response his superiors sent Lawrence back to England on the first ship. A few years later, at the age of 45, he would die in motorcycle accident while riding on a narrow English country road. He was avoiding two boys who were biking in the center on a sharp curve. Lawrence fell on his head and died soon after: If his elbow had intervened, he would have lived—such is fate. Once again, he achieved sensational press around the planet. Someone has said that the news of his death reached the same frenzy as Princess Diane's death in August 1997 in Paris. Strange to say, but there are similarities between these two doomed celebrities. While they longed for privacy and dignity, they also lusted after recognition and fame. And both were charismatic, foolish, and brave.

TWELVE

WALLY'S WORLD

Walter Vanrenen as a young cavalry officer in the
British Indian army.

This photo depicts a gala event, a Raj celebration with banners, marching bands, and cavalry in their finest. These marches and parades were very popular in the Raj days, part of the propaganda and the fun. The photo was taken by Walter, probably around 1938. His caption reads that these people are part of the Viceroy's entourage.

Wally's family had been in India a long time (since 1781), when a young cadet traveled from South Africa to India. Jacob, my grandfather (x4), went there to find a new life. He had been orphaned, adopted by a British sea captain, and went to England with this kind man. That is, in short, how a branch of the Van Rhenans became anglicized, resulting in the spelling Vanrenen. Jacob would lose his adopted father and return a sad young lad to South Africa to find his fortune. He had no parents, few opportunities, and no money.

His story, the adventure of his life as a soldier in India, came down to me from my great (x2) grandfather, John Henning Vanrenen, colonel in the British Indian cavalry. His son, Adrian, wrote down notes from a history his father shared with him, a cornerstone of Vanrenen mythology. And I received a copy of his notes that tell the story of Jacob's emigration to India from South Africa, a young cadet and orphan, looking for a new life. Well, he most certainly found a new life in India, achieving success in the ranks and retiring as a brigadier general. He had married, fathered nine children, one of whom was my great (x2) grandfather. Jacob would die and be buried near the sacred Ganges.

The East India Company, a large and powerful trading concern—in fact, a multinational giant of the time—was extremely powerful in India, overseeing trade, warehouses, shipping, and conquering. They operated out of London. Jacob was one of many young men who joined the East India Company as a soldier, sailor, or merchant to try their fortune in India.

In 1870 in America, the young ambitious men and women went west. In the British Isles, these people often went east, mainly to India. Jacob lived at a time when the British Indian Empire was expanding at an alarming rate. They would fight at least one major war every decade as they marched across the great land. Jacob was, one can say without reserve, one hell of a tough dude. How many men have served in an army for 50 years, with barely a furlough?

A rare and well-preserved studio shot of Jacobs's great-grandson, my great-grandfather, Jacob Peter Denys, a colonel in the Fifth Cavalry. Incredibly enough, this well-preserved photograph is around 140 years old. Jacob and his family lived in military towns in

Northern India—the British called these cantonments. Each was a world of its own cut off from the swirl of Indian life! They had their servants, cooks, and gardeners who were, for the most part, Indian. Wally and Zizza would experience the twilight of this strange era. Of Jacob Peter I know very little, but he looks very familiar!

A treasured photo, over 140 years old, of the Fifth Cavalry, with great-grandfather in the center, colonel of a tough bunch of cavalry officers. You just did not mess with these guys. For recreation, they speared wild boar, hunted tigers, and played polo—a rough and dangerous game on horse. For their profession, they raised cavalry regiments and trained them to ride, keep order, and, when called upon, to kill. Highly proficient horse riders, they were skilled with saber, pistol, and rifle. They were the backbone of British might in India and formed almost invincible power in battle. All those swords they carry were not just for show. Battles (then and now) were ugly and brutal. But these men above, now long dead, are in the prime of their lives and proud to be a part of this elite force. They were handpicked, sifted through, and forced to train hard and persistently.

This is a rare younger photo of my grandfather Denys Henry, proudly displaying one of his champion horses at the magnificent stables at Renala. Even a person who knows nothing about race horses can see that this beautiful animal is a cut above the rest. Grandad wears the pith helmet that the British Indian men favored because it offered protection from the sun and from falls off the polo pony. The helmets were also a badge of distinction. He was a stocky, strong man, driven and hard-working, and not too easy-going. My grandfather was always on the move, motivated by the ambition of his male heirs and the ghost of his great-grandfather, Jacob, who had achieved legendary status in his world.

A former cavalry officer from a family of cavalry officers, Denys Henry was raised by a colonel in the 5th Cavalry under hard conditions. He endured years of discipline, starting as a young boy when he was sent "home" to England for school. But he loved his horses. He was a horse man and a master at care and breeding . In the days prior to the automobile, horses were paramount for transportation, recreation, and farming, and also for fighting. A big strong horse weighing over 1000 pounds, carrying a well-trained cavalry officer, armed with sword and pistol and whip, was a formidable opponent in war. Even more formidable were 200 trained horsemen in a tight charge, swords drawn, horses galloping, and pistols ready. It was futile to flee, often futile to defend oneself.

Wally's father's prime role in the army was to provide new and fresh horses, which is why it was called the Remount Unit. Horses were killed in war just like men, they were grievously injured, and they grew old. At the peak of his career he was the deputy chief of the Remount Unit in the Northwest Frontier.

Wally's world in India, by any standard, was exotic and different, a time that seems far removed from our own. It is hard for me to believe that my father, whom I knew much of my adult life, had been an officer in the British cavalry. In his thirties, he was stationed in India in lonely outposts, seeking recreation in polo and hunting and having fun with chatter and beer in the military mess halls.

For a time, Zizza was a part of this world, a drastic change from what she had known in Kent, England. She, cheerful and friendly, flowed through Wally's world with ease. Most people who came in contact with her liked her. She could adapt to all people and a variety of unusual situations and was exposed to a variety of "adventures" that few would take on. One of those adventures, a journey with Uncle Louis into the remote province of Ladak in the Himalayas, was the stuff of intrepid explorers.

This is a picture of DV, as my grandfather was known, receiving a cup—quite a big one at that, at a horse racing event in Lahore. I do not know who the lady is, but she looks suitably important, lady somebody. You can just hear her clipped posh accent: "Jolly good show, Major Vanrenen, and we will see you next year, won't we." The lady, no doubt, lived in a big mansion with many servants, and spent hot summers at the mountain retreat in Simla, attending gala dinners at the club, playing a little bridge, and going to tennis matches. And when needed, she would hand out a few silver cups!

There are a considerable number of hounds in this photograph. Four hunters. The British were passionate about their sport, and in India they could indulge in exotic sports like tiger and wild boar hunting. Wild boar hunting often involved dogs and a cruel chase. The boars, however, armed with sharp tusks and powerful body could be dangerous and fierce and would sometimes charge horse and rider, The British Indians, in their brusque way, called this violent sport pig sticking because the prime weapon was a long lance.

In the old days, India was a different place: an exotic land whose jungles teemed with wild animals, including tiger, deer, bear, boar, elephant, and panther, as well as an astonishing array of insects and snakes, including cobras, tarantulas, and a host of stinging bugs. There were birds by the millions, all kinds including exotic peacocks, doves, hawks, and parrots. And, of course, there was the ubiquitous monkey. Often housed in sacred temples, monkeys still live without fear of harm and occasionally harass visitors for food.

By contrast, today India is a country dominated by humanity.

In the 1930s, Jim Corbett, a British hunter and naturalist, became famous for his life and books. He tracked and shot rogue tigers who had taken to eating humans. He earned no fee for his heroism. An exceptionally brave man, he often went out alone at night to "sit," often in a tree, waiting for the tiger to come to the bait, sometimes a live goat tied at the base of the tree. Corbett earned the gratitude of the local Indian villagers who might be terrorized by a tiger for months.

On the other side were the macho British elite, who could go out to slaughter wild animals: birds, boar, tigers, deer, and bear. With the people of power—including rich Indians—elephants were used in tiger hunts. Of course, while riding an elephant, there was little to fear.

One account claims that a British lord and his companion, an Indian Maharaja, went out with thirty men and four elephants and some tracking dogs. They would hunt down and circle the poor tiger, who would attempt to charge out of the circle, to no avail. At the end of the expedition, thirty tigers were lined up on the ground for the photographers.

This senseless slaughter was not just carried out by British or Indians but happened elsewhere, like the American West. I can see three forces driving this extravagant cruelty: little egos trying to become bigger, boredom, and brazen greed. What was tragically lacking was a feeling for the life and wonder of these creatures, who have just as much right to roam as we do. And, sadly, it is not just the rich and privileged—of any race—who engage in this brutal slaughter then and now.

I love this photo, because in my collection it is the only action shot of polo; the central figure is my father.

Polo was the signature sport of British India. One had to have money to purchase the right horse and pay for its upkeep; you had to be an excellent horseman; you had to be able to hit a small, hard ball with a polo stick (which had a kind of wooden hammer on the end); and you did this while riding at top speed surrounded by other players also trying to do the same thing. You wore a helmet for good reason. It took much practice to become proficient. The goal was to hit the ball into the opponent's goal. The opposition would do their best to stop you and your fellow players. Polo is a team sport with strategy and passing. Your fellow players could be your best friend or your worst enemies, but for the most part there was much camaraderie. Wally's best friend was Willy Turner, a crack polo player whose face can be seen in quite a few photographs. Polo, however, was not a British invention, far from it.

Polo has an ancient Persian origin. There was a time when Persia had a fabulous empire that influenced India and the Middle East. Polo traveled to India before the days of the British, then was adopted by the British cavalry. A rough Afghan version exists, involving two teams of horsemen. A dead goat is thrown into the center of the field, and the idea is to score a goal by carrying the dead goat across the opponent's line. Unlike British polo, this version has few rules, and in rough games some players can die.

The British India version of polo involved four players on each team and a goal at each end of the field. A point was scored when the little, hard ball, hit by the polo mallet by a man riding a horse, went into the goal. Each period was a chukka, and there were four chukkas. Polo required riding skills; it also required money to purchase and train a horse or two and have time to practice. Of course, the typical cavalryman, when he got down to serious polo, was already an excellent rider. Polo is not a safe sport. You can fall off the horse; get hit by the hooves of a big, powerful horse; and get wacked inadvertently by a mallet.

In the British era, polo matches were very popular, and every region had their champion regiment team and their champions. It was like the thrill of Major League Baseball. Many of the cavalry regiments would form their own teams, practice, and then take on the rivals. Polo was part of the atmosphere of competition and power, and after the matches there would be lots of drinking, fraternizing, and laughing. And, I might add, at the club, much flirting. The ladies would swoon when the champion strutted by in his high leather boots. The cavalry loved their fancy uniforms, and some of the regiments even took to wearing turbans. Turbans, the head gear of Indians, became cool. In some situations, privileged Indians played with the British, and it became popular to play with one of these jaunty Indians, who were highly skilled.

In modern times, polo is still played in India and Pakistan and in many other countries of the world. The Argentinians, introduced to polo by English settlers, took to the sport with an extraordinary passion. My only experience with polo was a match I witnessed in Cowdry Park, England when I was a teen. It must have been an important match because the Queen and her entourage were there;

that interested me more than the actual polo. My father was never a man to tell stories, so I never heard anything from him about the game. But the photographs tell a story. For a while, in the young heated days of the cavalry, he loved it all.

I very much like this photo, partly because I "found" and rescued it. It was a tiny photo, barely noticeable, one of many. It depicts a particular moment in my father's life: a rest in between chukkas (a period) in a polo tournament with Wally, wearing hat and dark glasses, sitting in the middle next to Barbara Eddy, and on the left a burrah sahib (proper gentleman) called Dartmouth. It is a specific moment in time. Someone was there with a camera and snapped the shot. Those in the photo are not that concerned about being photographed, with the exception of Barbara, who always had her eye on the camera. Naturally flirtatious, she liked the company of men. Wally wears his polo outfit, with the scarf and hat (they did not wear those hats in the game), sun glasses, and a cigarette. Dartmouth looks sharply at the camera, mildly annoyed. I do not know his full name, only that he was a proper British aristocrat who was out in India for a little "adventure." He was hobnobbing with the colonials, a bunch of good chaps who rode a good ride, played a fine chukka, and raised the glass with a smile. I was amused to "discover" this photograph, as I had not seen an image of Dartmouth before.

My second middle name is Dartmouth, and my mother once told me with a laugh that they had named me this in the hope that I would one day acquire a small portion of Dartmouth's wealth. This never happened! I don't know what happened to this man. Some would die in the coming war, and, in fact, World War II was a terrible event for India and the rest of Asia. The Japanese sped across Asia with a zeal that took the British by surprise. Their little jewel of Singapore, a major port, was overrun by the Japanese. It is said that at the time of conquest some of the British officers were still playing tennis and drinking gin. Tragically, men, women, and children were captured by the enemy and sent to wretched camps. We have all read the books or seen great movies like *Bridge Over the River Kwai*. Wally and Zizza had friends who were interned in Japanese prisoner of war camps during the war. Many never returned. Was this Dartmouth's fate? I cannot remember what my mother told me.

The above photo is a classic British India image. Wally is on the right, with that darned dog behind him. The dachshund, a Vanrenen dog, Gaffy Waffy, must have

been a character—there on the polo field! I am sure some of the people in the stands were laughing. My mother used to mention the sweet, little dog. I remember a story she told me about Gaffy Waffy. At lonely Renala during the war, Ysobel and Zizza spent good times together: Ysobel had lost her husband, and Zizza had temporarily lost hers. One night, the little dog got up and wandered the upstairs bedroom halls, whimpering. Zizza and Ysobel got up to console the poor dog and see if there was anything wrong. Eventually they all went back to sleep. In a week or so, they found out that a close friend of the family, someone who lived at Renala, had died in the European war on that very night.

In the above photo—one of the few that Wally displayed on the wall—we see that his team has just won a monstrous cup in a polo tournament. On the left is a handsome fellow much admired by men and women for his riding skills and looks. He could have played James Bond. His name, which I heard from time to time, was Willy Turner, and he was a good friend of Wallys' and Zizzas'. I have no idea about what came of him after it all transpired. Then, as now, it was a precarious world with drastic social and economic changes every few years. British India would soon be rocked by riots, the independence movement, the dark shadow of World War II, and within two years, the end of the Raj. It just died one day, keeled over like an old whale, amidst Indian festivities, all presided over by an elegant British aristocrat, Lord Louis Mountbatten.

A cocky Wally in the garden at Renala, wearing his polo and riding outfit, perhaps ready to go to a tournament. A moment in time, with shadows on the horizon. In a year or two, off to war.

This is my only shot of Wally's regiment, the Central India Horse, with the wives there!
You can spot Zizza because she is the only person facing the wrong direction! That,
by the way, was emblematic of her (and my) life. Wally is to the right of her, with
one man in between. The colonel, the important and serious fellow, is sitting dead
center. Wally, according to my mother, had some serious disagreements with him—
something preferable to avoid in the circumstances— and, for most of his adult life,
Wally was known for his temper.

Loyalty and obedience were obvious virtues in the cavalry, and one did what was told: end of story. Men were cashiered (dismissed in disgrace); some got overly drunk; and some even accosted their superiors—and faced very harsh punishment, sometimes death. But for the most part, the army in India was a well-run machine. Wally, in the end, did not fit into the rigid discipline and pecking order.

Strange to contemplate: This was a day when all in the photo were living and breathing. Now all are gone. They dreamed it. It seemed real, and I suppose for a moment it was.

The letter below is from the Viceroy of India, Lord Archibald Perceval Wavell, writing to my grandfather Denys Henry about horse business. It seems that Grandad leased him a race horse, for which the Viceroy was most grateful. Wavell would become a general in World War II, a Field Marshall, and would be the second-to-last Viceroy, replaced by the flashier Lord Louis Mountbatten. General Wavell had an extraordinary career, serving Britain in several wars including World Wars I and II. The rugged old general displayed another side toward the end of his long and eventful life. He would publish a book of collected poems, Other Men's Flowers. *As for his role in India, Churchill did not like him, because he was not ruthless enough in suppressing independence.*

VICEREGAL LODGE.
DELHI.

The 1st April 1929.

Dear Major Van Heems

       I have only just heard that 'Richmond Bell'

went back to you some ten days ago, and you must

have thought it very rude of me not having written

to you beforehand.

       It gave me much pleasure having her, and she

really is a very nice mare. I only wish there had

been more horses in Delhi for her to try her metal

against. It seems hard to make racing a success

in Delhi, and had it not been for your generosity

in sending down these fillies, I do not think we

should have carried on at all.

       If prospects seem brighter next year, and you

decide to send any more horses down on more or less

similar conditions, I hope you will give me the

option of leasing one again.

       With many thanks.

122

This formal shot, a unit of the cavalry troop, shows them in their finest. They had adopted the Indian turban, but not just any old turban. Their boots, for one, required careful polishing by the valet, and the turban had to be a certain pattern and set just right on the head. Willy Turner is noted, as he was a very close friend, standing second from left. Wally is standing in back on the second from the right, next to the one man who has forgotten his turban! I can just hear the commander bellowing:
"Davidson, where the bloody hell is your turban?"

This was how a cavalry officer and his lady got married. You can see the bride in the carriage. Wally is on the horse on the right, wearing his turban. Willy Turner, once again, is on the horse on the left.

A fascinating photo from my father's collection: It displays the grandeur of the Raj! These are some big shots, top of the pecking order, at a gala occasion. The British Raj liked to show off, demonstrating its wealth, power, and prestige. Here was a highfalutin' event when all the powerful got together to congratulate each other, and all in their finest, with carriages and personal valets and drivers. The man in the top hat was a leading politician, Sir Henry Craik, from a family of politicians. You can just hear him in his throaty British upper crust accent: "Jolly good show, old chap. Very good of you to come." He lived in a palace with a valet and an army of servants. In every era, the rich and powerful have their entourage—it is all very expensive. One sees this extravagance with our current president, Mr. Trump, who just cannot muster the character of these people above. They might have been rich and even pompous, but they knew how to lead, many of them, with a sense of gravity and a compass of honesty.

ZETTE, WEDNESDAY, APRIL 1, 1

Sporting News.

(FROM OUR OWN CORRESPONDENTS.)

POINT-TO-POINT RACES AT RISALPUR.

The annual Risalpur Cavalry Brigade point-to-point races were held at Risalpur on the 16th and 18th of March; and closed the Peshawar Vale hunting and point-to-point season. This year again, the Master has shown us excellent sport. In Peshawar and some such as in Risalpur owe him a debt of gratitude for many delightful week ends. When one goes up to Peshawar, one is always sure of meeting many cheery fellows and of a jolly good hunt. Hounds came over to Risalpur on the 15th, and this closing meet resulted in an eight-mile point, the longest this season. The two days' racing provided some splendid sport. The course was as good a one as any man could wish to ride over, perfect grass country with plenty of sporting leaps. Captain Gell had taken an immense deal of trouble over the laying out of it and his efforts were heartily appreciated by us all, though some one was heard to mutter something about the quality of the water just before his soak for the third time in the double trench. Few people escaped a fall on the two days, but falling was soft and no damage was done, though, judging by the nasty black eye the Master had on the morning after the second day, he must have struck something harder than the rest of us. The second day was, unfortunately, very wet, but we are used to water (externally) in Peshawar, and few failed to turn out. Mrs. Blomfield, undeterred by the rain, motored over from Peshawar, and gave away the cups. The 13th and 14th Lancers dispensed hospitality on both days, the attendance on the second day being unfortunately diminished by the rain. Mrs. Turner, however, and all the ladies from Risalpur turned out and helped to make the day a great success despite the rain. Many of us could not help feeling sad as we rode home to think that we had come to the end of the season. But we cheered up later on when a large gathering collected for dinner in the 13th Lancers' Mess, and soon everybody was busy explaining how it was that they had not won the race. Details of the racing :—

FIRST DAY.

13th Lancers' Regimental Point-to-Point.

Mr. Connell's Larrikin, Owner 1
Captain Moody's Matchbox, Owner 2
Mr. Mayne's NewHaven, Owner ...

From the Military Gazette sporting news, announcing a "jolly good" day where all were cheery at the Raisalpur races, and where Birdwood, a Vanrenen horse, was a winner. These races and similar events were an important part of British Indian life and involved a lot of planning and executing. All empires, including our own, maintain their power through pomp and circumstance and a steady parade of events, sports, and propaganda. And some of it is fun!

Steeple chase with a Vanrenen on the lead horse. The British in India loved their horses, races, and sport, all of which were almost a religion to them.

This was a jolly good day at the Himalayan Men's Club, with Uncle Louis in front, second from right. He has his legs crossed, and he is not cradling a pipe. Four of the men have a pipe in their mouth! In front the officers, in back the Indian staff with their turbans: I suppose they took it all for granted. Let me say that the upper crust Indians can be just as snobby and elitist, then and now, as can almost all privileged people of any culture. Why are we humans so addicted to this kind of snobby behavior? Still, it was a jolly day, maybe for all of them!

A classic British India photo, with the two steely officers drinking a beer and the street urchin looking at the camera. I am sure he has already tried his hand at begging for money. This kind of scene is common in India today, the vivid depiction of poverty alongside wealth.

The British Indians, by the way, picked up their own Anglo-Indian way of speaking, which included quite a lot of Indian words. The proper gentlemen would be called *pukka* sahibs. Ysobel was the memsahib of Renala. The British, like my parents, inserted Indian words into their daily speech, making it colorful and original. They acted superior, but they were somewhat awed by the power of Mother India. For tea they said *chai*, for sugar *chinna*, and on and on. Some were peculiar phrases: my mother used to repeat (occasionally) the phrase: mutton, *roti, chinni, chai*. She probably picked this up from the cook.

The more privileged British had servants, cooks, cleaners, and even a boy to turn the fan—he was called the *punka walla*. Today, we have no idea how many people, of all types and classes, lusted after this lifestyle. Before the modern era, daily life involved much drudgery and mundane tasks: no washing machines, dish washers, flushing toilets, electric lights, stove, refrigerators, or phones. (I often laugh when I hear people today complain.) Officers, who could be terrible snobs, often had an Indian valet. They might act superior to these hard-working people, but they often developed friendships. Every English lad or lass growing up in India had an Indian ayah, who often became a close companion, much loved; naturally, the boy or girl would pick up Indian expressions and words and even habits. Mummy might be back in England for a prolonged visit or off at the club, but the ayah was always there. These Indians were sturdy and loyal people, some simple and often uneducated, but kind and considerate, and even the most hardened British sahib would sense this. Even my crusty old dad had some close Indian friends, Hindu and Muslim, with whom he corresponded with after he left India!

For those English who were in India for the long haul, the people and the land crept under their skin, and when independence came, though compelled by circumstance to leave, they retained a nostalgia for Mother India.

PRINCE AT THE RACES.

FINE WIN IN STEWARDS' CUP.

GREAT OVATION FROM THE CROWD.

A RUN WITH LAHORE HOUNDS.

(FROM OUR SPECIAL CORRESPONDENT.)

Lahore, Feb. 28.—Lahore runs quite a good pack of hounds and this morning His Royal Highness attended the meet at Shah-ki-koi. This morning owing to the lateness of the season and the exceptional height of the crops, the chances were with the jack, but one very good run was obtained which ended in a kill.

If the programme had been adhered to His Royal Highness would have paid a visit to the Cantonment after the meet there to inspect military pensioners, ex-service men and representative detachments of the units of the Lahore District, but this had to be postponed until to-morrow. In the afternoon His Royal Highness attended the Lahore Gymkhana races and rode in three of the eight events. There was a great crowd present and when the Prince motored down the course some time before the first race, he was given a great reception. In the Polo Scurry, the Prince rode Destiny and came in fourth. In the second event, the Lahore Cup, he met with no better success, but the tables were turned in the fourth event, the Stewards' Cup, when on Major Vanrenen's Jenny Wren, he came in a magnificent first with over a length in hand. As the Prince passed the post the most enthusiastic scenes ensued and he was cheered to the echo. In honour of the fact that to-day is the wedding day of Princess Mary the chief event of the day was styled the Princess Mary Plate. This was won by another of Major Vanrenen's horses, All Clear.

During the evening there was a small dinner and dance at Government House. His Royal Highness danced several dances, one with Miss Pamela Maclagan the youthful daughter of His Excellency the Governor.

CANARD EXPOSED.

INCIDENT BETWEEN DELHI AND

In 1926, India was honored by a visit by the Prince of Wales and his entourage. Later, the prince would become Edward VIII and then abdicate because he married an American woman, a divorced one. This all caused a lot of commotion in the government and public, but the truth is that the prince was not cut out to be a king. He was something of a charming playboy. On his tour of the empire, the prince stopped in Lahore to enjoy the races, where he witnessed the win in two separate races of horses owned and trained by Major Vanrenen. In fact, he would be riding one of the winners, Jenny Wren. He was given this horse for a good reason: It was a sure winner. The Lahore Racing Club did not want the prince to come in second place! "Damnation, give him Major Vanrenen's horse!"

The gala dinner afterwards was a posh occasion, and the prince took a moment to thank the major for the use of his horse. The prince, by the way, was a royal-looking fellow, exceedingly handsome and a lady's man. As said in the above article, after the dinner the prince danced several dances, one with the youthful daughter of his Excellency, the Governor. Dances, dinner parties, and extravagant fancy dress entertainments were very popular in the days of the Raj.

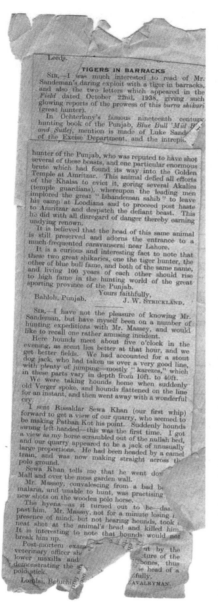

TIGERS IN BARRACKS

Sir,—I was much interested to read of Mr. Sandeman's daring exploit with a tiger in barracks, and also the two letters which appeared in the *Field* dated October 22nd, 1938, giving such glowing reports of the prowess of this *burra shikari* (great hunter).

In Ochterlony's famous nineteenth century hunting book of the Punjab, *Blue Bull 'Mid B'* *and Sutlej*, mention is made of Luke Sand' of the Excise Department, and the intrepi.

hunter of the Punjab, who was reputed to have shot several of these beasts, and one particular enormous brute which had found its way into the Golden Temple at Amritzar. This animal defied all efforts of the Khalsa to evict it, goring several Akalies (temple guardians), whereupon the leading men implored the great " Ishandeman sahib " to leave his camp at Loodiana and to proceed post haste to Amritzar and despatch the defiant beast. This he did with all disregard of danger thereby earning undying renown.

It is believed that the head of this same animal is still preserved and adorns the entrance to a much-frequented caravanserai near Lahore.

It is a curious and interesting fact to note that these two great shikaries, one the tiger hunter, the other of blue bull fame, and both of the same name, and living 100 years of each other should rise to high fame in the hunting world of the great sporting province of the Punjab.

Yours faithfully,
Bahloh, Punjab.   J. W. STRICKLAND.

Sir,—I have not the pleasure of knowing Mr. Sandeman, but have myself been on a number of hunting expeditions with Mr. Massey, and would like to recall one rather amusing incident.

Here hounds meet about five o'clock in the evening, as scent lies better at that hour, and we get better fields. We had accounted for a stout dog jack, who had taken us over a very good line, with plenty of jumping—mostly " karezes," which in these parts vary in depth from 10ft. to 40ft.

We were taking hounds home when suddenly old Verger spoke, and hounds flattened on the line for an instant, and then went away with a wonderful cry.

I sent Russaldar Sewa Khan (our first whip) forward to get a view of our quarry, who seemed to be making Pathan Kot his point. Swinging left-handed—this was the first time, I got a view as my horse scrambled out of the nullah bed, and our quarry appeared to be a jack of unusually large proportions. He had been headed by a camel train, and was now making straight across th' polo ground.

Sewa Khan tells me that he went dow Mall and over the mess garden wall.

Mr. Massey, convalescing from a bad b malaria, and unable to hunt, was practising new shots on the wooden polo horse.

The hyena—as it turned out to be—das past him. Mr. Massey, not for a minute losing i presence of mind, but not hearing hounds, took neat shot at the animal's head and killed him. It is interesting to note that hounds would not break him up.

Post-mortem exam   at by the veterinary officer sh   ture of the lower maxilla and   bones, thus demonstrating the   e head of a polo stick.   fully,

Lorālai, Beluchi   AVALRYMAN.

This newspaper article was tucked into my father's album. He must have treasured it for a reason: I suspect he knew one of the writers. It is very British Indian, an amusing article about a tiger that got into the barracks and how some brave officer scared it away. Yes, they actually had a tiger roaming the barracks. This was India in the old days. The British in India had their adventures. They also displayed humor, they had their close friends, and, sometimes, they shared a laugh.

I missed that time, as I was born in Africa several years after Wally and Zizza left India, but years later as a young lad I heard them talk about their good old friends in India. Much of this talk interested me, and I became familiar with names and saw their pictures and would hear stories (all too few). Often their friends had nicknames like Tiger White, Pinkie, and Jumbo, my uncle. So, strangely enough, even after my parents and British India—and all the players—are long gone, I can still recall their names and faces!

Willy Turner, spoken of with reverence as he was a great horseman; dark and handsome. John Gardener and his wife Sally, just good ole friends; blustering and large Tiger White; Halcyon Wright, the beauty of Gulmarg. "All the men chased her!" And she was gorgeous, dark-haired and slender and in one photo dressed in shorts!

I never asked my father what he felt about it all. (We did not talk much about feelings.) He was not a talkative fellow and never reminisced, and, furthermore, there had been some terrible experiences that he had to digest between that time and a better life in America. World War II, for example. Life in India in the cavalry, did it all seem like a dream? Was it a dream? It is as if he had been whisked off to another kingdom where everything was different, bathed in shimmering light, not all good, but very, very different.

Halcyon in charge of the situation, rifle in hand, on a hunting expedition in the mountains. Behind her, a large party of stunned or amused coolies. She was a great friend of my mother and Ysobel, and in their album, she appears in quite a few photographs. In this one, we see Halcyon in her element! She was not so keen on the drawing-room parties, bridge games, and cocktails; like Zizza, she preferred mountains, laughter, and adventure. Damn fine lady, that Halcyon, some of the men would have muttered over beer at the club—with some trepidation.

When a cavalry man married, he had to march through a gauntlet of swords with his bride! The above page is right from my father's photograph album. I was just a little boy in Rhodesia when I sat on his knee as he showed me some of these photos.

Wally had a brother (John, nicknamed Jumbo because he was so tall). In the photo above, we see Jumbo and Dorothy getting married, British Indian cavalry style. Wally and Jumbo were adventurous British colonials who would raise families in exotic countries. Jumbo and Dorothy had three children: Donald, David, and Vivienne, and after India, he would settle in at a vineyard in the beautiful hills above Cape Town, South Africa. Vanrenens had been instrumental in developing the South African wine industry. I met Jumbo's son

Donald, the same age as I am, several times. He had a fascinating career producing African music and currently lives in South Africa. Jumbo would retire to England with his second wife, Daphne.

Daphne, a very interesting woman, shared my interest in Sufism, Hindu spirituality, and meditation. Until quite recently we communicated via e-mail and letter, but at an advanced age she, dear Daphne, was becoming frail.

When a regiment, like the Central India Horse, had a fancy dinner, they went coat and tails, and no women! Not even an Indian servant in the main hall (that is, during the photograph). Wally is on the far right, easily distinguishable. After the war, Wally did not return to the cavalry. In World War II, cavalry was only for show, and for combat the cavalry officers rode in jeeps, trucks, or tanks. Gone were the days of the cavalry charging into battle with their swords and pistols! The last cavalry charge took place in the Northwest Frontier, around 1943.

This grand dinner represents the last supper: Soon, it all ended, the dream was over. The curtain went down, but how many of the players recognized that they were part of a show? That they were a part of a drama that would soon conclude? Was there another reality behind what was being projected? For some of these men, there would never be a high point like this, but others would go on, like my father, to create new lives somewhere else. And a few of these would even try to see what was behind the revolving stage of life that which we are all sucked into every day.

THIRTEEN

PEOPLE AND PLACES OF INDIA DURING THE RAJ

The British loved the Indian word "Raj," the king or ruler, as it so clearly depicted their grandiose ambitions. But India was a land of many people, all kinds, many wonderful places, and many customs and social situations, some very foreign to British sensibility.

Out of the Ysobel/Louis collection, this is one of my favorites, a lovely image of a young tribal girl on a wooden boat on a river in the mountains, Kashmir. This photograph, and a few others, fueled my interest to create this book— and not to give up.

Another iconic photo from Uncle Louis; on an expedition he penetrated Ladakh, a remote mountain kingdom. Here we see two men on an animal-skin raft on a lonely river in the middle of a vast mountain wilderness where there are no roads or towns.

This photo depicts a very common "peasant" scene in India: Thousands of dusty little villages stretched across the vast plains, in the hills, and in clearings of jungle. The mother and daughter are pounding wheat in a large wooden bowl. Like so many millions of Indians at the time, farming was their primary occupation, and hard work it was. Everything was done by hand, and tools were crude. There was no supermarket to run to, and all food was raised locally, but sometimes there was not enough of it. Periods of famine were not uncommon during times of war, unrest, or drought. In our present culture in the West, we, who are privileged, take all the gifts of creation and man for granted.

Ysobel colored this photograph of the river that runs through the scenic and popular, then and now, Srinagar in the Himalayas. You can see the houseboats, which were in great demand by tourists to rent, but for the locals a pleasant abode. Srinagar was close to the family hill station of Gulmarg.

A lone Indian fisherman on a lake in the Himalayas.

This peaceful image, enlarged from a tiny photograph, is like an impressionistic painting. It is dreamy, deeply spiritual, and imbued with silence.

One of the thrills I had when I first examined the photograph collection was a sense of discovery. What is next? Some of the photographs I initially ignored, only to go back and find something or someone of value and interest. Some were tiny, and when professionally enlarged and scanned, became a startling image. In his collection, Uncle Louis had over one hundred tiny photographs, an inch or more in diameter! A thoroughly impractical way to go! Many of these were unique shots—a few I have presented here—of his time spent in the war (1919) on the Northwest Frontier. Some were miniature shots of people, landscape, and buildings, and the few I chose to present here are of great interest. He had other kinds of photos as well, some that looked quite professional, of a wide range of subjects—as we have seen in this book.

Fishing in a lake in Kashmir. A moment in time. This photograph was Ysobel's magic.

Village scene. One of thousands of villages, then and now, where life is hard and has gone on much like the previous centuries—the never-ending labor to raise food.

A "native" celebration with the "straw" man, accompanied by music. A rare photo, circa 1928. India had (and has) many fabulous cults, celebrations, and secret places. One can only marvel at its many wonders: secret caves filled with ancient Buddhist art, temples carved from stone, tribal people living in the jungle, game parks with tigers and elephants, immense temples that are like mini cities filled with a thousand wonders, and many active living devotees. To the British, the above rural celebration was a curiosity, but to the locals it was an integral part of their passage through the year and their respect for the great and unseen forces of nature and life. Indians lived, as many people used to, in close relation to the seasons and the great wonders of life, seasons, nature, life, and death. People were not separate and superior but an integral part of the organic movement of life, on the earthly level and from above. And life in a village was not all drudgery. Seasonal celebrations could go on with music, dance, and festivities for several days.

A common sight in India in the old days. This is what made India so enchanting for those British who were adventurous. Before the arrival of vehicles such as trucks, the elephant was a worker, a valuable contributor to village and farm life, and the man who led the elephant developed a close relationship with his curious, large friend.

A delightful image: having tea in the mountains with a sadhu or wandering holy man. India was filled with these sights and people, still is, but foremost the Indians respected those intrepid men and women who sought life's mysteries and wonders, often wandering the roads and mountains with little on their backs.

In the mountains, there were many distinct tribes with their own language, ceremonies, and customs. Near Gulmarg, several mountain tribes lived off the land, some wandering like gypsies, setting up camps here and there. These roving "gypsies" were called Guchas, Zizza told me. They made quite an impression on her. She was not burdened by British snobbery but was always curious and friendly with the local people she met. For Zizza, gypsies were not aliens: in the old days in England, even during her youth, you could still see gypsy caravans in Kent, brightly painted, parked in the shade of generous oaks. European gypsies, it seems, originated in India and have maintained ancient traditions wherever they travel.

These are views of the route north as one approaches the hill resort of Gulmarg, a long and scenic trek into the mountains, but well worth the effort. Coming out of the hot plains of the Punjab, Zizza always felt a thrill of excitement and freedom, and Ysobel was always a cheerful and engaging companion.

The above photographs by my grandmother, also colored by her (there were no color photos in those days), show her love for the incredible beauty of the Himalaya Mountains. The inscriptions are in her hand, something I am happy to see: "Spring in the Happy Valley of Kashmir." This is a lovely place one can visit today; it attracts many visitors in late spring when the flowers come into a symphony of glory under the blue skies, and all around the snowy outlines of the most majestic mountain range on this planet.

In Gulmarg, many afternoons were spent wandering the valley with friends like Halcyon. A picnic would be arranged under a canopy: teatime, with fruit and crumpets. Happy hours spent admiring the flowers, mountains, and all the little wonders of nature like the birds and butterflies. All the worries of the Raj would drift away into unreality like gossamer fibers in the wind.

Here is a description of this flowery wonderland, written by Colonel Holdich from his book *Borders of India*: "The time for scarlet tulips to decorate the hillsides had come. They were there in patches of vermillion, and hung about the blue hill landscape in vivid contrast. Purple thistles and wild poppies and roses were of slightly later bloom; but there were, even then, beds of graceful white opium poppy, varied with slate-colored beauty, massed in patchwork about the feet of old gateways. The villages of the valleys were buried in orchards, now scattering their wealth of pink and white blossom lily to the passing winds. Lucerne beds were already knee-deep in luscious greenery, and the odor of the scented willow pervaded the moist, hot air."

I am very fond of this photo of three Indian fishermen on a lake in Kashmir, Northern India. It is faded but that increases the atmosphere. This certainly is a moment in time and the feeling of stillness, the water, and the symmetry of the men and mountains is quite extraordinary. Let us surmise that, somehow, the photographer, Ysobel, was invisible.

The above, from my father's collection, is not a great photograph, but a memorable image. This was a trip that Wally and Zizza took to the colorful province of Gujurat. Gandhi's family came from Gujurat. This impressive building is the maharajah's palace, rulers who lived in a high style. During the British days, the Maharaja's mini

kingdoms were allowed to exist within the larger domain of the British Indian Empire. They had no jurisdiction beyond their properties. Some were tiny, a palace and 40 acres, others were larger, and a few like little countries. The Maharajas fascinated the British because they lived in an ostentatious style, a relic of a dying medieval world. Some of these men were eccentrics. One had a pet tiger; others maintained harems. All had servants, cooks, butlers, drivers, and soldiers, who acted like a police force. Many were immensely wealthy, living off mineral wealth or the labor of their "serfs." Some were shrewd businessmen with generations of experience behind them of ruling and governing. Some became great sportsmen, polo players, and big-game hunters, and often parlayed with British top dogs. A few were scholars and lawyers trained in London. Often, in the more important "kingdoms," the British would post a civil servant to "watch" over things, and what an interesting experience this must have been.

It was remarkable that the British conquered and unified India. India, for centuries, had often been divided between different tribes, cultures, and political institutions. Warfare and conflict were the norm for hundreds of years as each region or state went out to conquer or built walls to protect themselves. But within the turmoil of changing history, the Hindu and Muslim culture reached peaks of accomplishment and art. The British arrived like visitors from another planet, and managed to unify the whole country, and in a way—with trains, telegraph, and roads—that had never been done before.

India, despite its social problems, had a layer of magic that was hard to overlook; it still exists: beautiful fabrics with colors that the British would not have imagined, intricate works of art, delicate and finely crafted, exotic temples, quixotic people of varying races, languages and culture, enchanting music and dance, very beautiful women and handsome men, and a rich and ancient history that long precedes the European. They also had a spiritual and intellectual heritage that was ancient and rich. Some British scholars surmise that the ancient written language of Sanskrit is superior to any European.

The analytic brain, the forte of the Europeans, often overlooked some profound facts of life; but it also afforded the British and others superiority in science, technology, and warfare. That division, however, no longer holds true as India has long since bounded into the "modern" world—with all its strengths and weaknesses, and dangers.

In India the British left many monuments: train stations which were like palaces, elegant government buildings, law courts, and stone churches. Throughout India, the British built hundreds of large ornate buildings in mixed architectural style, some a real hodgepodge, and most of them functional. They rarely built something for the sake of sacred feeling, to inspire awe and wonder to those who visited. While many are outstanding, if over the top, they could never match, in my opinion, the extraordinary beauty of the great Muslim or Hindu masterworks. The Asian art recognized the underlying harmony that is shared throughout nature, heart, and mind. The greatest Asian art is often an astonishing fusion of the two minds--analytical and intuitive—that we all share. Modern Western art has, for the most part, lost the sense of sacred which is, perhaps, our most important faculty—and the root of all authentic religion and spirituality.

This photo, which I took with a tiny Minolta camera that I could hide in my pocket, is an immense temple in the great southern city of Madras. There are some architectural wonders in the world, but few Western people have heard or seen the great temple complexes of Southern India, a product of a unique culture and vision. This immense tower is one of four, each at the center of one of the four sides, and it also serves as an entrance into a maze of rooms, sacred pools, sculptures, and dark corridors. No photograph could ever do justice to this massive monument of carved stone.

I remember wandering through this extraordinary complex—teeming with devout people, not a museum—in a state of wonder. Coming down a corridor with Johnna, we are suddenly confronted by a marching wedding ceremony, with the bride and groom riding a dressed-up camel, amid monkeys in finery and dancers in dazzling outfits. They followed a troop of musicians, all decked up in shimmering costumes, playing flutes and drums. We stepped aside, mouths open. Was it possible that India still exhibited scenes out of some long distant fairy tale?

The towers are nine stories high and covered with hundreds of painted statues of everything on the planet! Astonishing is not even an appropriate adjective. One enters the temple from a street lined with ladies—dressed in bright saris—selling garlands of flowers for the worshippers: one moves through a tunnel-like entrance and out into the maze of the complex, an intended representation of the universe itself. Equally amazing were all the people who came to the temple for contemplation, refreshment, and spiritual endeavors.

A rare and exotic photograph of a Buddhist Lama (center and calm) with his fellow monks, some displaying their musical instruments and masks (for dances). The date is around 1940, and the location is a monastery in Ladhak, a province in the Himalayas of Northern India. Ladhak, cut off from the modern world, was entered on foot, yak, or donkey over a high mountain pass. It has much in common with its neighbor, Tibet: situated in high mountain valleys surrounded by extremely rugged mountains; populated by a small number of shepherds, farmers, monks, and roaming traders; and subject to long, cold winters.

This photograph was taken by Uncle Louis, who had an adventurous (and spiritual) streak. He made several long excursions into the Himalayas, and one into Ladhak, which very few Europeans had visited. It was a long, challenging trek, but no doubt Uncle Louis had his bearers and guides. The bearers would carry all the food, tents, and cloths on their backs. Incredibly enough, Zizza went with him on this particular adventure. As with so many events, I wish I could ask her more questions. They stopped at this monastery in Ladhak where the local Buddhists graciously accepted to be photographed. The Lama in the center is an interesting man: you can see that he is calm and intelligent. He also looks quite young. Today, Tibetan Buddhism is familiar to many because of the Dali Lama and because China has occupied Tibet, driving out many of the Buddhists.

As a youth, from time to time, I would share something precious with my quiet—and sometimes distant— father. I remember those rare times when we would sit on the couch and he would flip through the pages of the family photograph albums, pointing our this and that. The photographs, like the one above, fascinated me, and made a deep impression on my imagination—in a time before we had a television or even much access to modern magazines. When televisions came into everyday American life, Wally refused to bring one into the house. I am forever grateful for his crusty, old-fashioned attitudes: my early years were spent creating games and playing outside—in many ways I had an idyllic childhood.

The journey into Ladakh was an incredible experience for Zizza, the young lady from a village in Kent. She was 22 in 1940 while war was raging in Europe. That is not to say the British in India did not suffer serious consequences of the war. For five years, Zizza was a war "widow" as Wally was stationed in Africa and Burma, suffering the horrors of warfare in the desert and the jungle. Zizza spent some time at a lonely Renala with Ysobel, or in the mountains at Gulmarg. The two spent good times together. But there was always the fear that a letter would arrive announcing Wally's death. This waiting was not easy, far from it, but at least she was distracted by the baby and her mother-in-law, and the expedition into Ladakh.

During that time, Zizza would travel to the War Office in Lahore and help out in the intelligence bureau, intercepting messages from Afghani and Indian sympathizers to Hitler. She worked, as well, as a code breaker. During the war, Zizza also had a baby (Val), who was born in a lovely hill station, Ootacamund, in Southern India. They called the place Ooty for short; it is known for its moderate temperatures, gardens, and lakes. Many Indians or British have passed through this enchanting place—its ambience lingers long in the heart.

India is a huge country composed of deserts, vast agricultural plains, mountains, and many different kinds of people with at least four major languages and 400 dialects. Even now there are primitive people living in jungles. Jungles, however, have shrunk considerably in the modern era, and most of India is deforested and crowded.

This is a page from my father's photograph album. His photos are more conventional than Ysobel's or Louis', but always of interest.

The India of British India was different from the modern India: for one, there were far fewer people. India today is second to China in overpopulation, and it is a huge problem. British India had far more wild animals and places and was a simpler country with fewer cities and paved roads and thousands of little villages populated with farmers. The British created a gigantic railway system that united the huge country for the first time and allowed common folk to travel, trade, and visit new places.

The British ruling classes lived in a strange Asian environment—strange for them—that included a hot tropical climate, foreign customs and religions, and a huge mass of Indians who were far removed from British ways. A group of privileged Indians became educated in British schools, worked in government or business, and became quite anglophile, and it was from this class that the independence movement emerged. Given the chance, Indians could prove themselves in science and government, and excelled in many fields of study including technology.

During the dream of British India, the privileged English had a secret passion. For many, it was delightful to get away into the cool hills with mountain views and fresh breezes, far from the noise and bustle of the plains. And here they could retreat from their responsibilities and the burdensome reality of empire. And in these hills, wherever they were, they created the illusion of a little England with gardens, tennis courts, cottages, and clubs. Ysobel and my family treasured their little sanctuary in the Himalayan foothills, Gulmarg.

FOURTEEN

GULMARG: THE MOUNTAIN RESORT

Separating India from the rest of Asia is the massive mountain range of the Himalayas. This mountain range and its neighboring ranges is the most impressive on the planet and contains the tallest mountains, including the famous Everest. K2—Karakoram 2—is in the adjoining Karakoram range and is the second highest; it is said to be the hardest mountain in the world to ascend because of extreme winds and abysmal cold. K2 is, in short, a death trap for the modern climber. None of the locals have been interested in ascension. The locals consider the Western obsession with climbing to the top of mountains somewhat strange. To them, the mountains are sacred, not in a mental or sentimental way, but in essential feeling and vision.

The Himalayan foothills, two hours north of Renala, were a popular destination for the British. In the summer, temperatures at Renala could reach 110° F. With no air conditioning, the only cool would be in the early morning. People slept on verandas under mosquito netting, and they drank a lot of fluid. Even ice was rare. In summer, the only respite was to head north.

A premier destination for my family was the beautiful village of Gulmarg, nestled in a cup-like valley in the Himalayas. Its name means "valley of flowers," an apt name because the valley and surrounding hills are brimming with flowers in the spring. At over 7000 feet, Gulmarg exists in another world, surrounded by majestic peaks, hills covered with pines and flowers, and cool fresh air. Furthermore, as the British often did in their colonies around the planet, they created a little English village with an elegant hotel, dining rooms, stone Anglican churches, quaint homes and cottages, and attractive walkways with flowers and bushes. But that was not quite enough: three golf courses, with one especially for women, as well as tennis courts, and, of course, riding stables.

My grandmother, Ysobel, was fond of Gulmarg and spent much time there in the war years with my mother—a war widow—and often walked her dogs, painted, and rode in the hills. She was sporty like her daughter Hazel, a local golf and tennis champion. Hazel, confident and pretty, was often feted at the club, but Ysobel liked her quietness, out on the veranda with a view of the great peak, Nanga Parabat. She was a good amateur painter and often added quick sketches to her notebooks, like a painting journal. I am lucky to own one of her more polished paintings that depicts her little Gulmarg cottage, her sanctuary for many years.

Gulmarg matches any resort in the world for beauty and weather, with one difference: it adjoins the most impressive mountain range on the planet. Today, the British are long gone, but middle-class Indians visit during the summer months to idle some time away in the cool air. The Indian government also created a top winter resort in Gulmarg complete with ski slopes and trails, and it is rated quite highly.

Geographically, Gulmarg is in the Indian province of Kashmir, now cut off from nearby Pakistan. The resort is around fifty miles from the picturesque city of Srinagar, a favorite tourist destination for many decades. Kashmir and Gulmarg were adversely affected by a dirty little war after independence when Pakistan sent irregulars and troops to take over the mostly Muslim province. This venture failed and peace resumed, but the region is still haunted by recurring incidents of violence, as is Pakistan itself.

During the British era, Kashmir was favored by the English, and Simla was the most famous resort, the premier destination for the bigwigs. Important politicians resided in Simla during the heat of summer, and for over one hundred years, important messages went out from Simla to London and major cities in India. Because Gulmarg was so important to my grandmother and family for several decades, I can present some lovely photographs. Its ambience resides in my heart, as it resides in the memory of anyone who has spent time there. Ysobel's love of her quaint little cottage, with the tall pines behind, is an image close to my heart.

The experience of the Himalayan mountains was one of the most satisfying for the British in India. And for those who have spent quality time there, the memory remains fresh. Lawrence Durrell, the English writer, born in the lovely mountain town of Darjeeling—famous for its tea estates—never forgot his early memories, even though his

Ysobel's cottage on the hill above the mountain village of Gulmarg. She loved this place, as did my mother; it was a sanctuary from the heat and commotion of India. It was also far away from the political realities of India.

family left when he was young. What is it that calls us? Something in the clarity and stunning beauty of mountains brings us back to our essential self. And when we really see them, feel them, our busy minds are silenced.

Ysobel's painting of her cottage, her favorite place in the world, above Gulmarg. On the back it says "Abdul Karem studios in Lahore." Abdul would attend her funeral: The two shared a love for photography and painting, and he gave her advice about cameras and photography.

After eighty-five years, the painting is in good shape, having been under glass all that time. It traveled from Gulmarg to Renala, by train to a ship in the port of Karachi, over the Indian Ocean, thousands of miles, to Cape Town, South Africa, north through the Kalahari Desert to Salisbury, Rhodesia, then by car to a tobacco farm, where it was admired for seven years, then back onto a train to Cape Town, on a Union Castle Line to Southampton, England—over 10,000 miles—on to my Aunt Mary's house, briefly, in Midhurst, Sussex, then back to the Queen Elizabeth at the docks in Southampton, across the Atlantic (in an old-fashioned canvas trunk) to the Cunard docks at Manhattan, then by car to Tuxedo Park, New York, hung on the living room wall for 10 years, then back into a truck to Boulder, Colorado, the living room wall, and then ended up—with stops in between—in Pembroke, Massachusetts, where I presently live. Imagine, if the painting could speak, the stories it would tell.

In the old days, prior to motor, the British traveled to Gulmarg by horse, carriage, and with a small army of "coolies" to carry all their gear. Here is a picture of the rugged route to Gulmarg and those tough men who for a pittance carried supplies into the mountains. In the 1920s, a rough road was built and the British would have their "drivers," often a Sikh, haul them up to Gulmarg in a car—quite an event.

Once, Zizza told me about a wild ride with a Sikh driver and Ysobel on their way to Gulmarg. An eagle happened to fly into the car. The windows were open and Zizza suddenly had an eagle on her lap. The driver stopped, got out, opened the back door, and shooed the stunned bird away. Ysobel laughed, and said: "Zizza, what kind of omen was that?" And off they went to the picturesque wooden cottage, on the hills overlooking the mountain resort of Gulmarg. They would paint and walk together, maybe play a little golf and fraternize at the local club, have teatime on the porch with the dogs, and late afternoon strolls over the flowering meadows. This was a sanctuary where the heat and realities of the plains of India, of Renala, drifted away for a short time.

Another image, by Ysobel, of Happy Valley and the flowering lilies, with snow-dusted peaks in the background. Farms in the valleys abound with fruit trees, and the local people live a healthy life fed by the fertile gardens and the heavenly ambience.

One of my favorite photographs. Hazel, Wally's charismatic sister, and Zizza enjoying a day at the cottage in Gulmarg. Hazel, on the left, was a beautiful lady, full of humor, chatter, and life. She enlivened any party and was always engaged in activities including championship golf and tennis. On this day, however, Ysobel asked her to sit down and pose, which she readily did. She and Zizza are enjoying the company of six dogs, warm sunshine, and cool mountain breezes. This was a different world from Renala, which was flat, hot, and in the midst of the busy Punjab. Zizza is managing three dogs, including the charmer, the dachshund, Gaffy Waffy. Somehow this little dog made it into many photographs.

Ysobel and Zizza, and many others, loved the view from the cottage of the famous mountain Nanga Parbat. They both painted this scene. The majesty and wonder of the Himalayas could not help but enchant even the most hardened heart. From the hill resort of Gulmarg in Kashmir, one could see the magnificent white crests of the highest mountains in the world.

A photo of a wooden bridge in the exotic, mountainous state of Kashmir. Kashmir, in the Himalayan north, is a land of wonder, fine people, and great physical beauty. In the rear toward the right, one can see the outline of what looks like a Buddhist pagoda.

Once independent and mostly Muslim, Kashmir became incorporated into the modern Indian state, partially through the influence of Nehru, who had family roots in Kashmir. Nehru, India's first leader, was a Hindu and refused to allow Kashmir to become a part of Muslim Pakistan. This resulted in war, small battles, and perpetual acts of terrorism (or political liberation—depending on your view). Today, life there is quite peaceful, despite an "incident" now and then. Lurking, however, beneath the surface are old wounds and frustrations, similar to Afghanistan and the Middle East.

Tea time in the mountains with the locals. A curious picture, mysterious because I know nothing about the people or the occasion. I am guessing that the two men on the right with the turbans are local maharajas. The two on the left are wandering sadhus, definitely local mountain people. Certainly, this is a mountain picnic, but it is unknown who in my family is attending, and I don't know if Ysobel or Louis took the photograph.

One of my favorite photos by Uncle Louis, who had an observant eye like his sister-in-law, Ysobel. A lone Indian contemplates the mountain creek with the great Himalayas as a background; this is an iconic symbol of the contemplative side of Indian culture. What is hidden beneath the surface of ego chatter, worry, and noise? This photo asks this question and does not expect an answer.

FIFTEEN

RENALA; YSOBEL AND LOUIS

Renala—from Ren, as in Van-renen—is the name of the Vanrenen home and estate in India—today in Pakistan. Renala is no longer; it is a ruin, rather the ghost of a ruin. Located in the prosperous state of Punjab, Renala is about one hour south of Lahore. It was founded by Major Denys Henry Vanrenen, Wally's father, in 1913. DV, as he was called, was a captain in the British Indian cavalry, the elite forces that kept peace in that great empire. Before the jeep and the truck, the horse was important in law and order and in warfare, and the British Indian cavalry was one of the best in history.

A respected horseman, DV was commissioned by the army to found a horse farm to breed and train the best horses for the British Indian cavalry. He and his fellow soldiers searched the region for a suitable place. They chose an area of primitive scrub jungle where they could direct a small canal—very important—and convert the scrappy land into rich farmland, fields, and even a village (where laborers and farmers would live). In the center they placed the impressive colonial house and gardens, where the captain and his memsahib would live with their young, growing family and their workers. Nearby were paddocks and barns for the horses, houses for the staff and administrators, and a village for the workers.

Wally, his brother John, and his two sisters, Doris and Hazel, would spend their younger years in Renala, along with their parents, the formidable DV and his charming wife, Ysobel. Ysobel came from an English-Scottish family called the Butlers, who owned a tea estate in Assam. Ysobel's maternal grandmother, a German related to Baron Von Poelnitz of Germany, was an impressive matriarch who lived to age 102.

DV—as he was known—was a solid English fellow who had deep roots in India. His father and grandfather had been cavalrymen in elite regiments stationed all over India. In those days, there were legendary regiments like John Brown's cavalry; Central India Horse (Wally's regiment); and the Bengal Lancers. In 1935, Hollywood released an adventure movie called the *Lives of the Bengal Lancers*, one of over twenty movies with these themes. In this movie, Gary Cooper attempts to protect the British interests from wild and unruly natives. It had a famous director, Henry Hathaway, and good cast, and won seven Academy Awards. All these Frontier movies, whether in the Northwest Frontier or the American West, show the steely dominance of a few white heroes over a mass of dark-skinned savages.

In the British days, every cavalry regiment had its uniforms, prestige, and reputation. Every one featured polo teams that trained regularly, and its crack polo players were the stars of the day. For power, prestige, and mobility, the horse was king.

Renala had another distinction: it was close to the infamous Afghan border—then and now a region of unrest, warfare, and conflict. The best horses went to the regiments that policed the dangerous border of the Northwest Frontier. By the mid-1920s, Renala was an estate that bred some of the best horses in the country: It had its beautiful gardens that were presided over by Ysobel Vanrenen; it was visited by local officials and famous visitors, and was sometimes the scene of gala events, horse races, cocktail parties, and fine dinners. DV introduced quality horse breeding into India, and in time his horses would be champions and much coveted.

My father was notably quiet about his past, so I rarely heard stories about his life in India. However, when I was young, he would show me his cherished photograph collection. I do not remember his telling me a single story about his father. This whole period of his life was colored by such mixed emotions that he preferred, despite many good experiences, not to indulge in stories. Furthermore, World War II, five long years, was a terrible final chapter to his "Indian" years.

I should add, however, that though Wally was a reticent man, he was not shy or antisocial. All his life he liked people and had a string of friends from continent to continent! He was also a charmer with the ladies, and that devilish smile did not extinguish until his last day. However, he was not an easy man to live with, sometimes angry, and, I believe, hurt that he had never fully expressed his talents in life. He was sorry too that he had not had a "real" college experience. There was a touching period when in his elder years he attended, briefly, a community college. I remember that Wally and Zizza's friends, where ever they lived, were interesting, even charming people.

About her India experience Zizza told me some stories, and I wish I had asked her much more. I remember her telling me about a dinner at Renala when top officials and local landowners came to dine and socialize. Everyone wore their finest, and the dining area was decorated to the maximum. Servants were on high alert, especially the cooks. DV and Ysobel were the proud hosts. Of the forty or so guests, each had an assigned seat. Zizza found herself next to a quiet, unassuming man, a guest from New Delhi, capital of British India. They chatted lightly, he charmed by this lovely, slightly giddy lady. Weather was a popular topic in India, as were horse racing and polo, and at dinners political problems (or as the British would say, troubles) were rarely discussed. Zizza told her middle-aged dining companion about Renala, the gardens, farms, and horses. After the dinner, a friend came up, took her elbow and led her into the veranda. It turned out that Zizza had been chatting with the Viceroy of India, Lord Archibald Wavell. The notable fellow had an interest in grandfather's race horses, but despite his high position he was a pleasant, humble fellow. The flashier, domineering Lord Louis Mountbatten would replace him as the last viceroy of India.

All was not serious in British India, which is why I love this photo of three good friends in a very friendly pose. There was no notation beneath the photograph, so I do not know who they are but good friends with Wally and Zizza and, judging from their clothes, they are going riding. During the hot season at Renala, they would ride early in the morning. And even the British enjoyed siesta in the afternoon, with tea or iced gin. Noel Coward, the song writer, would coin the phrase: "Only mad dogs and Englishmen go out in the midday sun."

Noel Coward, the famous playwright, came from Kent, the same area as Zizza, and sometimes the little girls would see the distinguished, gay fellow drive by in his fancy automobile. Coward was a great talent whose songs and plays enlivened the British stage in the period between the wars, and even in India, local English groups would stage his musicals. The British, despite their reputation for seriousness, had a good sense of humor and loved song and dance. Both Indians and the British in India had a long tradition of fancy dress, plays, and musicals. I don't think Wally or Zizza ever put on costumes and pranced around a stage singing Noel Coward comedy pieces, but most likely some of their friends did.

A view of the main building at Renala. The magnificent gardens were an oasis in what had once been—not so long ago—a scrub jungle. Photos of the buildings are, for some reason, rare.

A rare photo of the Renala gardens, Ysobel's creation with her Indian gardeners. Renala brimmed with help: cooks, gardeners, stable hands, and house boys. These good people were treated well, and many would remain faithful to the end and would even express regrets when the end came. One cannot applaud this lavish lifestyle in our age of democracy, but even today the wealthy Indians have their servants. The reality of castes lives on in this ancient land.

A quick sketch of the Renala gardens, painted by Ysobel, an avid gardener, and the memsahib of Renala. In the region, her gardens were well known. They impressed not only because of their color and design, but also because the surrounding area was so wild and straggly. Furthermore, the local Indian aristocrats had a long tradition of beautiful gardens laid out with water courses, fountains, and flower beds—all to represent paradise. Ysobel tuned into this vision.

Renala was all about horses. Even if you didn't ride, you must have your photo sitting on a horse! This photo, from around 1939, is an image of my uncle and aunt: David Ronald, Zizza's brother, who visited Renala with his wife, Lizzie. David was in the British Army but stationed in many different places, with a position in NATO after the war in Naples, Italy. Upon retiring as a colonel, he would receive major awards for his service.

A copy of a page in Uncle Louis' album. The upper photo depicts a dignified lady in a carriage; who she is I do not know, but she could well be a player in a BBC series on British India. The lady on the Renala horse is also a mystery but most likely a friend of Uncle Louis, because there are two photos of her on this page. Some of the British women loved to ride (and not side saddle). The sporty British had their entertainments that distracted them from some of the profound questions of life. They were living in a land where people had examined themselves and life for thousands of years. In fact, India was and is a fertile ground for philosophy, religion, and art.

Zizza in her riding clothes in the gardens of Renala. She was allergic to horses! Imagine. There she was living on a horse farm with a very horsey family. But she gamely tried to ride every so often, taking her hankie with her. She loved spending time with Ysobel, and the two would go up to Kashmir to paint and admire the mountains and flowers. There were not many horses up there!

This beautiful horse was a reason for Renala's existence: Olivestone, a champion, with his Indian handler, was one of DV's great racers, and he had quite a few. In the photograph albums, there are numerous photographs of horses! The studs were a very

important part of Renala, and many made a name for themselves, valued over a large region, even overseas. When a horse was a proven winner, when it had good genes, it was a good idea to pass these on to the next generation.

There is a complicated art and science to horse breeding, a discipline at which my grandfather was a respected expert. And as any animal lover knows, the animal responds far better to someone who understands, cares, and respects them. The horse whisperer is none other than a man or woman who can relate to the animal as a friend. My grandfather, I know, respected the Indian horsemen who worked with him and fed, exercised, and cared for the great mares and stallions. To the horse, there is no race, sex, or religion which he will favor! He or she instinctively knows, even better than some humans, what someone feels toward him or her.

Sister Cal, as a youngster riding a tricycle, was born at a hospital in Lahore in 1946, just after the end of World War II. She would end up living on five continents and marry an Englishman, Alex Horsely. They had three children, my nephew and nieces Dylan, Natasha, and Anita, with whom I share friendship.

The Horselys are a northern English family, probably of Viking stock, like the Ronalds. In the eighth and ninth centuries, Vikings from Scandinavia raided and conquered, settling in the eastern portions of England. Migration, trade, and conquest have been two huge influences on human life and culture, no different today as then, and so true for the history of England and India. The strange and sudden appearance of the British in India is no anomaly, and, in fact, India had been run over from time to time by foreign people. The "original" Indians—the Aryans—probably rushed through Afghanistan like so many conquerors after them.

Zizza with her first born, my sister Valerie. Years later Val would marry Richard Belmont from New Orleans and give birth in Denver, Colorado to two children, Roderick and Vivienne. After the premature death of their mother, Rod and Viv would be cared for by Zizza. In this picture of Zizza, you see the beauty of the English women, from Viking and Anglo-Saxon genes, but singular beauty is found in all races and countries. India, with quite a few racial types, has its generous share of beauty, from the dark-skinned Dravidians of the south, always slender and fine-featured, to the diverse tribal women of the northern mountains, who were short and petite with high cheek bones and raven black hair.

I love the photo on the left, so old-fashioned, but who she is I do not know. Perhaps she is one of the family— a cousin, or a girlfriend of Uncle Louis. He remained a bachelor his whole life, but judging from the photos in his photo album, he liked the ladies very much. He was a shy but handsome fellow, not as outgoing as his brother, my grandfather. The photo on the right: Uncle Louis at a young age, perhaps twenty, with two serious women. The approximate date of this ghostly but lovely photo is 1910.

After India became the Raj, a major part of the great British Empire, the government back home instituted a policy to send women out to India. There was concern that the English men in India might fraternize with the Indian women too much! In the early days of British presence in India, "cohabitation" with the "native" women was frowned upon by the rulers and the Church. Of course, it was not uncommon.

In time, boatloads of English women landed at the major ports of India to be greeted by a local church committee of kindly men and women. After they were settled, they would be presented to the male society at local church dances. There were occasions when bonds occurred quickly, and marriage vows settled the affair after the dust had settled. These must have been touching occasions with the nervous ladies dressed in their best—accompanied by a chaperone–and the shy but eager British gentleman. And there must have been sad occasions when some shy lady did not find a suitor, and vice versa. This isolation would be especially hard in India, and more so for the woman than a man, as there were more jobs for men regardless of marital status.

Uncle Louis, who was not bereft of lady friends, never married and worked hard as the manager of a large indigo estate in the Sind province. When he retired because of ill health, his Indian workers sent him a letter expressing their thanks for many years of good leadership. I have a copy of this letter, and it is long and sympathetic. Life must have been hot and lonely on his estate in the middle of nowhere, but he did not have far to go for a holiday; the ships at near-by Karachi to take him to France, or the train north to Renala, and beyond that his beloved Himalayas.

Uncle Louis loved travel and adventure and trekked into the Himalayas a number of times. He hunted big game too, but he was not an avid hunter. He did not like killing animals, as you might see from his expression in the above photograph. He was good with a camera and probably used one of the good German cameras of that time. Occasionally, he went to the port at Karachi and took a ship to France—a place the Vanrenens love—to spend a week or so in Paris: and judging from all the pretty female faces, he was not too lonely. But none of the French or English women were able to pin him down. Ysobel would say: "A confirmed old bachelor, and there is nothing we can do!" She would throw up her hands and laugh.

"Dear, dear, Louis," Ysobel once said over afternoon tea in the garden, "When are you going to get married?" He did not reply, just gave a little smile. "What about that Henderson girl, you know Molly? Her father is a prosperous planter. Yes, what about her, a strapping lady! I saw her looking your way at the tennis last Sunday!" He looked at Ysobel and smiled. "No, I don't think so, Ysobel. She's a lovely sort of girl, good sport and all that, but … not really my type." "Dear, dear, Louis, who exactly is your type?"

Jolly good day relaxing in the living room at Renala: cigarette and ice gin with lime. This very comfortable gent, whose name I do not know, is one of the managers of the large estate of farms, horses, barns, fields of produce, paddocks, a crew of workers, main buildings, villages, and gardens. Renala was a big enterprise that even published an occasional booklet about its properties and activities.

Ysobel loved Renala and Gulmarg. Like her husband's brother, Louis, she was modest and sensitive and loved nature, art, and people, which is why some of these photographs are special.

175

This lovely faded copy of a photograph is my only image of Ysobel as a young woman. Donald, my cousin in South Africa, sent me the image a few years back.

This photograph of Ysobel and Uncle Louis in the gardens of Renala is striking. She looks unflinchingly at the camera, grounded and steady. She has the demeanor of someone who is poised and quiet inside, generations of a centered presence. Uncle Louis looks more like anyone getting photographed, a little distracted and looking away, but he, too, has a presence. After all, he is in her aura!

They loved the countryside, the beauty and adventure of India, particularly Kashmir and the mountains. Both took some wonderful photographs. Ysobel would never speak harshly or mistreat anyone, British or Indian. Ysobel and Louis, careful observers of life, displayed their artistry in the photographs. For amateur photographers, they had an unusual eye open to the transcendent image. And there was nothing of an "empire" stance in their art, no pretension or posturing.

Ysobel was down to earth, close to nature, and an aspiring painter. She also shared a streak that runs through the family from time to time: a mystical sense of oneness with nature. You can see that in her expression and in her best photographs.

Little did these smiling people know, but their era was about to end. Ysobel, second from right, at a later age, standing next to her husband, one of the few photos of them together. On the left is Jumbo, my uncle, and next to him a lady I do not know. They are in the Renala gardens, circa 1936. Wally and Zizza are not yet married. I met Jumbo a few times and always had a good impression of him. He was a warm, outgoing man. As an old man in his eighties, he would live out his years in England. Jumbo's second wife, Daphne, was a remarkable lady whose family were British Indians. Years later she would tell me that she and Jumbo met in South Africa, almost by chance, but their families in India had known each other for years. It was one of those meetings sparked by synchronicity.

Even until five years ago, I would, from time to time, communicate with Daphne, Jumbo's wife, via letter and e-mail. She had become interested in Sufism in her later years and was a writer of some distinction. Some in my family—Caroline and Wally—would study and respect the spiritual paths of Asia: Sufism is a wise and deeply spiritual branch of the Islamic religion. Sufis meditate, engage in sacred dance, and meet often to support their path in life. Some of the great Sufis are also poets of remarkable skill. Rumi, one their luminaries, is a world-famous poet. And in India, we have the luminary, a woman called Rabia, who became a much-loved poetess. Formerly a princess, she took to the roads singing, dancing, and creating, in time, a legend.

I don't think the British Indians read much Sufi poetry or Indian spiritual texts about life and purpose. But today these kinds of books are popular in England, America, and many other countries. And, more importantly, the practice of meditation, mindfulness, greater awareness of self, and yoga have permeated Western society.

This is a perfect British India image! A lady with Uncle Louis on the tennis court at Renala. Neither is dressed for tennis. He might have just returned from an early morning ride, she from a refreshing cup of tea on the veranda. She was eager for some attention from him, the distinguished bachelor whom nobody had been able to "catch."

The extraordinary fact about most privileged British women in India is that they did not have a lot to do: cooks, cleaners, and valets did much of the work. And generally, they did not have jobs in the world. Some, like Ysobel, were far from idle: She minded the staff and kitchen, tended the gardens, planned social events, painted, and traveled, particularly to Gulmarg, and she participated in altruistic societies.

Some of the British women participated in what they called "good" works for the Indian: teaching, medical care, and feeding. The indomitable Annie Besant, who was one of a kind, actively engaged in the Indian freedom movement. She, not a "proper" British Indian, raised many eyebrows, and completely went against the "norms" of her society. Besant, who had a remarkable life, would go on to become one of the founders of theosophy, the first "new age" spiritual movement!

I do not know of any British woman who was prominent in the army or Indian politics. In the Hindu, Muslim, and British societies of India, women were second tier, though respected. Shiva, the Hindu goddess, is an important archetype in India. The British—and the Indians—had their beloved Queen Victoria, one of the great monarchs of English history. Mohammed, the prophet, was married to a woman who helped him establish his illustrious career—in Islam there is an important female precedent. And as I said, there is the much-loved Indian mystical poetess, Rabia. Daphne, my aunt, would contribute to a book about Rabia, a Sufi saint and poetess.

When the British first came into Pakistan (a part of India then), the social structure was feudal: many peasants, the ruling class, who were the major land owners, and in between a small number of merchants, officers, and civil servants. The British became the upper, upper class, but the aristocrats of the three main societies—Hindu, Muslim, and British—were alike in many ways, and, more or less on the same tier.

Uncle Louis with an Indian friend, both being forced into a photograph by someone in the family. Louis had many Indian colleagues and friends, as did many of the British. This fellow, whose name is Mohammed Khan, was also friends with Wally, Ysobel, and Zizza. He was a Muslim, as many in the region were, and a Khan (signifying a lord and land owner). He also knew horses. Years later, he and Wally would correspond, even when Wally, in his later years, lived in America. I still have one of the letters this kind man wrote to my father in 1970. It is most touching that Wally and this man were close friends for so many years.

I found this curious sketch in the back of Ysobel's painting sketch pad. It showed another side of her, playful and creative. It shows, also, that she was not only a British Indian matron, but a lady of the continent. Her maternal grandmother was German, and in her youth and elder years, she spent time in Paris and Southern France. My grandfather DV is buried in a little village near Cannes. Both my brother and cousin David owned French vineyards. This place keeps drawing all of us back. It is a curious thing, these interests that we all share, from whatever family, and to whatever place or activity or sport.

A moment in time, one afternoon in Renala, on the great Indian subcontinent, circa 1937, Ysobel and one of her gardeners in the garden alcove in Renala. She wanted him—whose name I do not know—in the center. He, however, is shy. She tried to defer to him; he is most devoted to her. She is the memsahib, but relaxed, kindly, and at ease.

Village scene in the mountains, painted by Ysobel. Many of her paintings were quick sketches in her traveling notebook, painted while she was on the go! They do not have the fine finish or polish, but were more like a visual journal. I don't know how many of her polished paintings survived, but I am fortunate to possess one, of her cottage in Gulmarg.

MONTE CARLO

Ysobel and DV vacationed in Southern France. This is her rendering of a little place called Monte Carlo! In 1926 she and two friends took a walking tour of this region, and she carried a painter's notebook, which she filled with sketches, including the ones of Renala above. I am lucky to have received this treasure from my father.

Even the ageless and courageous are susceptible to traumas, emotional pain, and old age. This photo of Ysobel, or as she came to be called, Granny Van, shows her not long before her tragic death. She is in Gulmarg with her two beloved dogs. At this point, the war against the Nazis has ended, and she is a widow and looks sadder than in any photo I have seen of her. There was a lot to be sad about. Her husband had died of complications from a horse riding accident. The great indomitable DV, who had risen to the top, was gone. Her world was coming apart as the British era was ending. She was thinking of going back to England or staying at Renala. Her enterprising daughter, Hazel, was determined to stay at Renala and run the whole damned place. Ysobel had another fate.

I insert this page straight from Ysobel's photograph album to show what it looked like. Some of these photos, enlarged, have been displayed elsewhere in this book. Top left is the beautiful Halcyon Wright, the belle of India, and as my mother once said, "very popular with the men." She said this without a tinge of jealousy. Zizza was herself quite a beauty, but very few could compare with Halcyon, who was not the stuffy British Indian warhorse; she was beautiful, humorous, flirtatious, friendly, and adventurous. She was not averse to trekking in the mountains or riding horses or playing golf at Gulmarg or going to the local club to be surrounded by all those handsome cavalrymen. I look at her picture with curiosity: Whatever happened to this woman? Was she married? Where did she move after the British vacated India in 1947? She was close to Zizza and Ysobel.

Even Halcyon needed help climbing up the steep hills around Gulmarg, but here she might be posing with her two "shikaris." One of the men carries two guns for this most adventurous woman. In the picture below, somewhat faded, she is second from right, off with a group of friends on a riding expedition into the mountains around Gulmarg.

On a lake near Gulmarg, the sunset over the distant hills, an evening like so many,
another to enjoy and savor.

The last days of British India came right on the heels of World War II. The British were worn out and the Indians, led by Gandhi, were crying for liberation. During the war, even the diehards had to admit that India was going, and after the war, the timetable for independence sped up, baffling some of the British. There were times when even the mighty British went to sleep.

These were hard times for Ysobel and the family. It was an emotional, uncertain time at Renala. Ysobel had lost her husband. The indomitable DV had had a horse riding accident, broken his hip, and at the time doctors used X-rays with abandon, thinking they were curative and diagnostic. From the X-rays, he contracted cancer and died in 1938 in Southern France where he had gone to recuperate. Zizza never met him, but his shadow lingered on at Renala and in the family.

After independence, Ysobel elected to stay on with her daughter Hazel, who had taken over running Renala with her husband, Jack

Taylor (a man I know very little about). Zizza mentioned him in passing. Ysobel visited England and family, returned to India via ship, and when taking the train back to Renala, disaster struck.

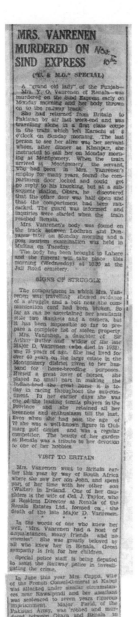

Left is a notice of Ysobel's tragic death, murdered by robbers on a train. The times were uncertain, only a year after the violent partition of India. When the train reached her station, her carriage was empty and there were signs of a struggle. Officials then rode back along the tracks and found her body.

In the notice she is called the "grand dame" of the Punjab, a fitting title for a woman who many knew and loved, British and Indian. As my mother told me, robbers boarded the train from horses and chose her carriage as it was a private one—good prospects. She resisted, as she was a tough old bird, and they threw the elderly woman off the train. What can you say about people like that? It is so sad that this fine lady with such a distinguished life would have to end like this. The news must have been terrible for the whole family, and for Wally and Zizza, who at the time had already departed from India for a new life somewhere else.

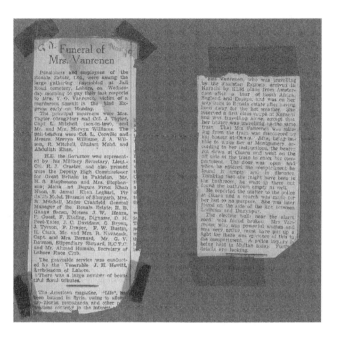

Here we have the announcement of her funeral, which was attended by friends, family, and government representatives. The esteemed deputy High Commissioner of Pakistan was there, as well as a representative of the governor. Also attending was my Uncle Mervin Williams—whom I admired as a young boy—with his wife Mary, Zizza's sister—whom I would get to know twenty years later in England, and also an old family friend, Ghulam Mohammed, whose picture is in the section on Uncle Louis. The other Muslim name is interesting: Abdulah Khan owned a photography shop in Lahore, and it was fitting that he would be here to give his regards to his old friend, Ysobel, who visited his shop many times to purchase cameras and film, to have photos developed, and to have paintings framed. Perhaps Abdulah was one of the secrets behind the artistry in Uncle Louis' and Ysobel's photos.

This was truly the end of an era: for my family, colonial India, the British presence there, and the beginning of an era for Pakistan, independent India, and for Wally and Zizza, who were off to another continent, actually three continents—but not all at the same time.

SIXTEEN

HAZEL AND THE END OF RENALA

Inevitably, Renala would die; all people and places are subject to mortality. Renala had a relatively short life, somewhat the same length of a hearty old man or woman. It was pioneered from scrub jungle by my grandfather in 1913, and reached its zenith in the 1920s and 1930s, but it did—even in a steady decline—survive the disastrous partition of India when the estate would become a part of the new nation of Pakistan.

After my father left India on independence, Hazel, Wally's sister, and her husband, Jack Taylor, took over the estate. From my mother, I heard that this transition was far from easy: The four siblings struggled through this period after the untimely death of their father, then Ysobel, their beloved mother. What a time this must have been: the horrible World War II had ended, life begins to resume its more natural patterns, but in India the British acquiesce to independence that happens quicker than most expected—and slower than the Indians wanted. The British Indian Empire, the jewel in the crown, dies quite suddenly. It was the giant centerpiece of the British world empire. No other colony compared with India in age, grandeur, history, and people; no other colony was as large and as storied. It must have been a shock to some of the old-time British Indians, even if they had seen, for the past decade, the coming of a new order.

The Indians had been crying out for independence for several decades, led by the indomitable Gandhi—just the right person at the right time. Gandhi, deeply imbedded in Indian spirituality, was honest and honorable, more than the typical politician. He knew in his heart that India should and must rule itself. The British, even with their clumsy good intentions, would never understand India or Indians. Jawaharlai Nehru, the first Indian leader, once said that the British were a sensitive people, but in a foreign land they acted quite strangely. Some would argue that the British had done their job: the Herculean task of helping to bring India into the twentieth century. Some might groan at this, but the British introduced railroads, modern education, manufacturing, a universal postal service, and a pretty decent legal system—a mammoth task that took into consideration Muslim and Hindu concerns—and modern technology/science. Many of the great Indian liberation leaders attended universities in England. Even Gandhi, with his staff and simple clothing, had once been a London law student in a Savile Row suit and stylish haircut.

Unlike the masters of other empires, the British did not unleash a bloody war to retain their power. With reluctance and foot-dragging, they acquiesced to independence, displaying, in the end, a good measure of fairness and grace. Nehru, soon to be leader of the new India, would acknowledge this fact. Come mid-century, it was time for the British to go, and go they did, in droves. There really was no place for them as Indians filled the high ranks of army, government, and business. The British had already experienced how Indians, given opportunity, could be more than capable. Those few who remained were in trade, or, like Hazel, stubborn people who for love or eccentricity would not or could not leave.

It was not an easy transition with the horrors of partition and the expected pains of drastic but needed change. This was a hard labor, but a new nation, filled with pride, was born on August 15, 1947, overseen by the elegant Lord Louis Mountbatten, the last British viceroy of the Raj. The Punjab, one of the great provinces of India, and where Renala was, was tragically divided, wrenching for the Sikhs—a dominant presence there—and the Hindus and the Muslims. Over 10,000,000 were dislocated, and, in a tragedy of horrible proportions, over 1,000,000 were massacred.

Pakistan, a Muslim nation led by the shrewd politician Muhammad Ali Jinnah, would be born, and this is where Renala now existed. Jinnah was not a friend to Gandhi—far from it—and Mountbatten did not like the man, but he was a steely, determined leader who launched the almost impossible dreams of the Muslim League. For the Muslims of that region of India, it was a great achievement to have their own country. Once, during the Moghul era, they were lords of India; now they were a minority in a sea of Hindus. With Pakistan, they found pride and honor, but the way forward was a road paved with many stones and obstacles.

I know little about the feelings of the inhabitants at Renala as their world collapsed. My father never spoke of it, and I never asked him. A little over a year after independence, Ysobel was murdered on her return to Renala after visiting relatives in England. By then, Wally and Zizza had left India for good, along with Wally's brother Jumbo and sister Doris. Doris had lost her husband, Len Mitchell, in a wartime plane crash and she returned, heartbroken, to England. Doris, whom I never met, was the most fragile of the four siblings.

Wally and Zizza must have felt a host of emotions when they boarded an ocean liner for England with their two little daughters and trunks of belongings and clothes. In those trunks they carried precious artifacts from their life in India: carpets, statuettes (the laughing Buddha!), pictures, paintings, and wall hangings. There must have been some anger and grief in Wally, but perhaps some relief, and expectation of hope for a new life elsewhere—where, exactly, he did not know yet. In a few years he had lost his parents, Renala, his profession, and British India. And worst of all, he had spent almost five years in terrible war conditions, coming back shaken and wounded.

The end of his profession, the British Indian cavalry, was inevitable; coming back from the war, Wally had no more passion for soldiering. He wanted to be a farmer, a man of the earth, and not fussing all the time with the pecking order of army life. British India: This was a natural transition in the making for decades. Renala: that had been his parents' love, and he felt grief and sadness but was willing to move on because they were no longer there. The death of his mother, Ysobel, hit him hard. She was blessed with a gentle, patient nature that his father lacked (indeed, many Vanrenen males lacked patience). Generations of soldiering runs deep. Ysobel had been the beating heart of the family for all the siblings, for the extended family.

Zizza, of course, grieved over Ysobel's tragic death, but Zizza was not a British Indian, not in her heart or history, and, like me, felt no ties to grandeur, armies, and empire wars. Zizza was ready to move on, but no doubt, she was deeply moved by a range of emotions and must have had her hands full with all of Wally's changes. Through wrenching life changes, Zizza came through, a pattern she would maintain for her whole life. For Wally and Zizza, the chapter in India, that adventure, had ended. There was no going back—they were off to a new life…somewhere.

A very touching photo of Hazel, the sister of Wally. She was quite a lady, and in her prime tennis and golf Champion of Gulmarg and Northern India. Down to her bones, she was a British colonialist who fully believed in her mission and lot in life. Hazel, enterprising to the core, also owned a coffee plantation in the highlands of Kenya. After the Vanrenens left India, Hazel, her husband Jack, and her son John would stay on in a Muslim Pakistan. Her life, like that of Karen Blixen—who wrote Out of Africa—*could be a movie.*

Renala was not owned by the Vanrenens, but leased from the state, a 50-year lease ending in 1964. Hazel fought valiantly to extend the lease—for that there was a generous clause—struggling with a hostile government and hiring lawyers to stay on. This went on for some time and ended tragically. More on that development soon.

Hazel, a vivacious and sociable woman, also loved sport: horses, riding, golf, and tennis. She was also a horse lover, like her father, and a hard and capable worker. And she never wanted to give up Renala, perhaps in loyalty to her father. She gave her life to it...to the bitter and tragic end.

She and her son John stayed on, as well as her husband, Colonel Jack Taylor who was—for me—a shadowy fellow, except that he was resident director of Renala after the death of DV in 1938. I believe that Jack died not long after. Hazel loved Renala; she loved the horse business—that was still viable; and she did not want to give up her tiny corner of British India. But it was a precarious position, even though she was strong, stubborn, and very capable.

She knew Urdu, the language of Pakistan; she knew many high-ranking Pakistanis; and she had made a name for herself, a reputation. She was an unusual woman living in a world where women were second class—in the British, Hindu, and Muslim cultures. I get the feeling that one did not mess with this woman. At her side was her son, John, now a young man, also a great fan of Renala. So a miniature British India lingered for a while at Renala, complete with gardens, farms, main house, barn, and servants. India might be independent but the locals needed work, and many were loyal to the memsahib. Some would stay with her for forty years or more.

Post-independence (1947) Renala, amazingly enough, survived, if modestly. People still needed horses and mules, and there was still a small call for prized race horses. By the 1960s, it was still operational, but after that it was limping along. Hazel, the powerhouse, was now over sixty, and her tenure at Renala had been repeatedly challenged by hostile governments. It must have been a major annoyance for the officials in Lahore to be dealing—still—with a pushy colonial. But she

This photograph shows Hazel, on the left, in her prime, the golf champion of Northern India, and with her trophy and happy smile. The runner-up looks a little sour!

employed Pakistani lawyers and would go to court when the need came. She and John fought to maintain their control over Renala and its substantial acreage.

The birth of the new country, Pakistan, in 1947 had been a hard labor. Gandhi had opposed the division of mother India, but the Muslim front, led by the shrewd London trained lawyer, Jinnah, persevered. Post-independence, life in Pakistan was not easy for its citizens—despite the burst of initial optimism: government corruption, revolving governments, economic distress, Islamic extremism, bombs, assassinations, a war with India, and troubles in the Northwest Frontier—as usual. It was in this milieu that the aging Hazel struggled to keep Renala going.

My father had a distant relationship with Hazel, partly because they were separated by continents. From time to time, they would exchange postcards. I never met Hazel. Wally passed away in 1979, and my mother exchanged Christmas cards with Hazel and John every year. We heard strange rumors that Hazel and Renala were troubled and shaky. I remember, in the 1980s, hearing that local police had beaten up and injured John.

The battle grew dirtier. Local army and officials, perhaps greedy for the land, were sick of these annoying throwbacks. They wanted to take Renala from Hazel and John. They wanted the property. But they had a pair of jackals to contend with, and Pakistani lawyers and high government officials. Hazel had a reputation, and she had some Pakistani allies. Finally, the news from Pakistan came to a trickle. I assumed that old Hazel had died, and that John was managing by the seat of his pants. He had some of his mother in him. But was he still at Renala? Was he safe? That I could not find out. And what had happened to Renala?

The answers were almost impossible to obtain. Not one of my relatives in England or anywhere else knew any facts. I could not call John, I could not find a number. My address for him became obsolete. And I did not know anyone in Pakistan to whom I could write or ask. Pakistan, at the time, was in political turmoil; there were terrorists, Islamic extremists, and war across the border in Afghanistan. I even thought of flying to Lahore and checking things out on the ground. I was deeply tempted, despite the risks. The adventure of that journey did not happen, for a variety of reasons, but I did find out the facts from some unexpected sources. I found out what happened to Hazel—that was terrible news—Renala—more expected, and John, my cousin—not so bad after all. Renala, of course, had died, not such a good death.

On the Internet around 2004, I came across an article written by a Pakistani journalist (in *Shirazi*) about his travels in the region south of Lahore. This adventurous man was traveling around the countryside on his motorcycle. At one point, he stops at a gate to an old ruined estate: a messy, unkempt, and battered mansion. Interesting that he knows that this ruin was once the famous horse breeding estate of Major Denys Vanrenen. He sits there on his cycle, musing for a moment: a poignant monument to a passed era, one that had an influence on his young country.

Then around the same time I managed to get a letter through to cousin John and was pleased to receive two replies. John was perhaps the last living remnant—in Pakistan—of the British Indian Empire. Except for his posh education at Harrow and Cambridge in England, he had spent his whole life at Renala and Pakistan. He spoke the language; yes, he knew the people and country very well. But he was still a Brit and a part of him wanted out. But he was stymied. He could not return to England—and this could have been true of Hazel as well—because he had not been born there, and neither had his father, mother, or grandfathers. He could not get a passport! But another part of him still fantasized about resurrecting the Renala he had known. His letterhead was quite impressive with his long title and underneath: Of the Renala Estate Limited. John also claimed that he was friends with Princess Diana, who would get him permission to return to England. In the longer letter, he was beginning to ramble.

The only photograph I have of cousin John, as a young colonial boy standing next to Uncle Louis on a lake near Gulmarg. He was born in India, schooled in England, and worked at Renala much of his adult life. Louis has a spotting scope around his neck and is taking the young lad out to spot exotic birds. If only someone had had a movie camera that day and could have recorded their conversations, and stilted British accents! That day is now long gone. This day, as I write, will soon drift into the distant past. Strange, is it not?

I looked into John's situation, to try to find out what was going on and whether I could help him in any way. What were the facts? Somehow, I managed to send him an e-mail. On his letterhead he had an e-mail address and by now, e-mails were universal. A few years back they did not exist. He did not reply, but oddly enough, in time, I received a reply from a friend of his, an American. This was strange. His friend explained that she was an aid worker operating out of Lahore where she had met John at a local café. She had befriended John and hoped to help him. She described John as a little lost, disheveled, and confused; she shared her computer with John. John had shown her the e-mail from his American cousin. The friend also shared that John had a Pakistani partner who seemed to be taking advantage of John. John, like Hazel and Wally, had invested money in an international bank with offices in Lahore; he had some financial resources—no surprise, really. Well, apparently people were taking advantage of John. I had this image of this hunched-over, skinny, Anglo-Saxon elderly man wandering the streets of Lahore, an eccentric who was known and perhaps abused. I saw him in a tattered, slightly stained, two-piece suit. I tried to maintain a correspondence with this friend, who I knew was not a fake. The friend unexpectedly sent me an e-mail saying she was pulling out, afraid that she might come to harm from John's Pakistani partner who was very possessive (or greedy?). I would never hear from her again. John's e-mail became a dead issue, and I had no mailing address. He no longer had my home address. John did not respond to me anymore. The door had shut. He became a mystery, remains a mystery, and I don't even know if he is alive. If he is alive—in his seventies—I suspect he is living in Lahore, wandering the streets like a ghost—the last haunted remnant of the great British Indian Empire. He could be fantasizing about resurrecting Renala. John, in effect, was off the map.

Then, unexpectedly, in 2010 I learned something crucial about Hazel and Renala. At the same time from two sources, I found an interesting article by a Pakistani writer who had, incredibly enough, written a story about Renala in 1990. One source was my partner,

Lorraine, who is handy with research; the other came from a link from my cousin Donald, now back in South Africa. The source on the Internet came from a Pakistani journalist in Sajjanlahore, archives, issue 47, 1990. I will reproduce the most pertinent sections of this article. The capable writer Zafaryab Ahmed, to whom I am grateful, calls his article: *The Renala Estate Story*.

"I was excited about the prospect of having a chat with a colonial, when Tatti Bourdillion, a journalist friend, asked me if I could go with her to visit H.J. Taylor (Taylor was Hazel's last name), perhaps the only survivor of the raj in this part of the world. Throughout the journey from Lahore to Okara, I planned how I could make this woman of eighty talk to me about the days of the raj. I was interested in learning about so many things: her reasons for staying back when the British left, that too when most of her clientele were in parts of the subcontinent that constitute India ... such an enterprising lady with a total dedication to horse-breeding and the daughter of the man who had introduced that craft to the subcontinent ... One wanted to know whether she had miscalculated or whether she could not foresee the future relations between India and Pakistan. {These, by the way, had been far from good, including threats of war and actual battles—my note.} What kind of communal violence had been experienced in these areas? {During the violent months following the terrible partition of India and Pakistan in 1947—independence for two new nations!} What kind of relationship had she had with the local people? Where did she get labor for her farm? What was the attitude of the local gentry and big chiefs of the area toward her? All this and much more. Just to compare her experiences to what one read in history books? All this day dreaming turned into a nightmare. "The Renala Estate is located in the district of Okara 72 miles south of Lahore, just three miles from the railway station in the direct line between Karachi and Lahore line. It is a comfortable 90 minute drive from Lahore by car.... Mr. Vanrenen, a major in the British army, developed the farm. After his death, Major Vanrenen's daughter who was married to Col. Tayler took charge of the farm continued breeding good quality horses both for the army and commercial purposes. She had a good business until Mr. Desai's government decided to put a ban on Pakistani horses competing on Indian turf.

"There was no tradition of horse-breeding. Indian horses were of poor quality. During World War I, the deficiency was felt more acutely. Arab horses which were being used in India had degenerated....

"In 1912 Major D.H. Vanrenen suggested to the British colonial government to establish its own horse-breeding farm in India. He was allowed to set up a farm at any place he felt was suitable for the purpose....An area of 7,723 acres was first leased to him in 1913, initially for a period of 20 years, renewable in perpetuity for periods of 10 years. The lease also had to option to purchase the whole of the estate at the end of the lease term. This continued until May 1955 when the Government decided to withdraw the right of the lessee to purchase or obtain perpetual renewal.

{I add the following: This was followed by a long period of legal wrangling between the authorities and Mrs. Taylor, during which she was constantly threatened with removal. She prevailed. Differences were not settled, however, and her situation at Renala was, at best, precarious—particularly with revolving governments and periods of Islamic revival. In 1989, it looked like she had lost the battle.} Our writer goes on:

"This is where Mrs. Taylor's ordeal begins. Tatti Bourdillion, who has made friends with the old lady since her arrival in Pakistan is the only person who has been visiting her. 'Since the first week of my arrival in Pakistan' said Mrs. Bourdillion in reply to a question on the way to Okara, 'my friends one after the other told me about this old English lady whom they used to characterize as Ms. Haversham—a character from Charles Dickens's Great Expectations, an old lady who lives in a world of her own. Finally, I decided to visit her up at Renala. She was pleased to hear from me and invited me over. The following Friday I visited the farm and this became a regular thing for me,' she paused.

'Whenever Mrs. Taylor visited Lahore, she used to visit me and Iris Leghari—wife of Sardar Atta Mohammead Khan Leghari. Iris is exactly the same age as Hazel (Mrs. Taylor). She used to visit Lahore quite often. She used to stay at Falettis. (Falettis was a fashionable hotel in Lahore.) An outgoing person she enjoys meeting people. Hazel and Iris have been good friends for years.'

"Now this poor old lady is confined to one room of her home and is not allowed to move out. Her telephone has been disconnected. She has been totally detached from the outside world with army guards posted at her door. Talking to me Mrs. Taylor complained about not being able to go out and meet friends. This was one of the main points in Mrs. Taylor's life. Her son John's room has also been sealed. He was not allowed to meet his mother the last time he came to see her. She does not know where John is now. She keeps writing unposted letters to him. This is her major preoccupation in these days of 'house arrest.' You ask her anything and she keeps bringing up John. Even during these difficult days she retains her sense of humor…

"One Friday when I came to visit her she was not there. I was told she had been moved to a hospital in Okara. I visited her in the hospital and found her bruised and paranoid. She was worried someone might kill her," said Tatti Bourdillion.

"I reported the matter to the British High Commissioner and she was allowed to return to Renala. Ever since, I have had problems visiting her. I can't stay with her, the whole house is sealed. The last time I was here I had to sleep on the floor. The soldiers were rude to me….I thought it would be nice if you came along. Then I remembered that you had shown some interest in meeting Hazel when we last met," Bourdillion continued.

{The two friends continue to drive to Renala and arrive at the gate where there is an armed guard who is moderately hostile. The guard tells Ms. Bourdillion that she cannot see Mrs. Taylor. She replies that she has contacted the British Commissioner, the Home Secretary, and some secretary of the prime minister who okayed her visit.}

We moved toward Ms. Taylor's room. We knocked at her door, which was open because there were no bolts. Ms. Hazel Taylor was very pleased to see her two visitors. She said that her electricity had been restored ....She complained that her servants were being scared away. Within five minutes the cook, Soma, who had been with the Taylor's for 40 years, came running. He told Ms. Bourdillion that there were people outside who were threatening that they would get the guests arrested if they did not leave. She said they were going to try to scare us... Ms. Bourdillion was sobbing and crying in anguish. The driver asked the men for the car keys. After a while they gave us the keys. They did not say anything to me. Perhaps they had only orders to stop Ms. Boudullion. Perhaps they mistook me for a sahib, as the colonel later told me. The situation demanded that we leave immediately. Any attempt to argue would have been futile. ... {Ms. Bourdillion adds that when she tried to return to Hazel's room they "pinioned my arms and dragged me all over the place.}" It was obvious that she had suffered a lot. Her forearms bore blue marks and her feet were all muddied over.

"We decided to go to Okara and report the matter to the Deputy Commissioner before returning to Lahore. The second thing that I wanted to find out was Ms. Taylor's legal status. The Deputy Commissioner expressed his regrets and said he would take proper note of the matter after talking to the Colonel in charge of the regiment. {There is some back and forth with the officials who, obviously intend to do nothing. One official adds that Ms. Taylor is required to give them a list of her visitors—an odd request, but another tactic of harassment.}

Our writer concludes his story of Renala:

"Whatever happened at the Renala Estate Farm on June 21 leaves some fundamental questions to be answered by the authorities. What is Ms. Taylor's status? Is she under some kind of house arrest? If not, why is she not allowed visitors and attendants. If she has lost the court case regarding the farm lease why can't she be allowed to spend her remaining years in the house she has lived in all her life?

"The services of the Taylors, it must be remembered, are in many ways unique; they were pioneers in horse-breeding in the Sub-continent."

A lovely photograph of a young and vibrant Hazel holding my sister Val in the gardens of Renala. Note the little Dachshund in back; he or she managed to get into many photographs, even if only the backside. Ah, a day in the life of the three of them, a moment in time, now long gone, not even a dream for them. How precious life is, each day, each day; each day to wake and walk in gratitude.

So that was it! Mr. Ahmed, a fellow with a good heart, and the kind Tatti Bourdillion might have been the last civilized people that Hazel spoke to. Locked away at her age, abused, and not even allowed to see her son, she must have died soon after this ugly incident. What a terrible end for anyone. I doubt very much that I will find out anything more about her or John. I doubt very much that she was given a proper funeral or burial, and it is very unlikely that I could locate her gravesite, because it does not exist.

I am grateful to express my respect for her and her family. If she never had an honest and respectful burial, I am deeply sorry. But in my small way, in these photographs and words, I can create a memorial for her.

It is very strange but with her and Renala the last tiny bit of British India died. She was the last of a family that had first arrived in 1781; she was, as they say, the last of a breed. She had stubbornly held on.

Very stubbornly. And I wonder why she did. The time to leave had come and gone. Maybe she felt that she could not leave Renala. Maybe she had that feeling that some people get: an organic attachment to their little piece of Mother Earth. There is no doubt that Renala had died and had been gone for over thirty years.

My cousin Jean Mitchell, who now lives in Canada, spent some time in Renala as a young girl, and later went back for a visit after Hazel's death. What she witnessed was Renala as a near-abandoned ruin. Only very recently she told me a sad, ironic fact: Hazel had been buried under the tennis court. Former tennis champion comes to her final rest at an obscure unmarked grave on the court she used to practice on with such zest. {Strangely enough, another development in the saga of Renala just occurred, while this book is at the printers! In 2018 the Renala story refuses to end. My cousin Donald sent me a link to a story in a Pakistani paper written by a Dr. Ayesha Siddiqa. This esteemed journalist – in March 2018 – published a story about Hazel and Renala. Her fundamental question is why did Hazel not leave Pakistan before all her troubles? What was home for Hazel? At any rate, Dr. Siddiqa's article is a dramatic addition to the long and tragic saga of Hazel and Renala. Renala still exists! But it is a ruin. Ms. Siddiqa includes some touching photographs of Hazel's dusty shoe rack, the empty and filthy rooms, and even an antique dust covered car. What is particularly amazing – for the narrative of this story – is that the good woman stumbled across Hazel's grave site – a real marker still stands! Someone respected the death and passing of this incredible woman.}

Despite her tragic end, much of her long life was good, as she was blessed with a natural enthusiasm. In my own way, here, I have honored Hazel.

SEVENTEEN

DARSHAN

I was lucky enough to inherit two books that had belonged to Ysobel. One was a charming book of painted sketches, some I have presented in this book; the other, a spiritual book called, aptly, *The Riddle of Life*. From this, with its carefully underlined passages, I could tell that she was searching for a deeper meaning in life. The author, a Christian minister, is a sincere and articulate man who speaks of Christ consciousness not as something that belonged to one man. Christ consciousness is not an illusion but a state of enlivened awareness that people have sought after for centuries, something we can all strive for, even if in a small way. And it is not just an opportunity for Christians, but anyone with a sincere heart and effort to search: Muslim, Hindus, Sikhs, and those with no religion.

During the three centuries of British presence in India, few English people embarked on a study of Indian ideas, religion, art, or philosophy. They lived in their own "club," superior and above: some were curious, but more commonly disdainful. Of course, there were exceptions to this "standard." But, for the most part, the British stuck to their sports, Anglican Church, and clubs. Indian practices and ideas were off the map. India, a "backward" country, was filled with teachings, art, plays, music, architecture, religion, and philosophy.

While the British might have acted at times as interested tourists, there was an obscured understanding that the nation that they were occupying was saturated with creativity and wisdom.

Today, in America and Europe, everyone has heard of yoga, an import from India; everyone has heard of meditation and devotional chanting, both of which are still practiced in India and have been for thousands of years. The *Harvard Medical Newsletter* expounds on the value of yoga and meditation. While the British were in India, so many decades, few of them ventured to the local ashram or yoga studio, few delved into the repository of Indian philosophy, going back thousands of years, and few examined the intricacies of Indian religion, a vast field of study. The Muslim religion was thumbs down. Hinduism, the dominant branch, was labeled "heathen," and the Hindus an ignorant bunch who worshipped monkeys and cows. Hinduism is an extremely complex religion with many practices, devotions, and subsets, from peasants with their tiny altar of statues and incense, to huge crowds of devotional chanting, to intricacies of the Brahmin class and to subtle philosophy and practice meant to enhance this passage of life that we all share. From my perspective, I see that the core of Indian spirituality is quite clear and clean: a wish to find our place, to live well with others in this life, and to simplify all our acquired complexities of personality.

However, even in the early days of British India, there were British, sometimes called Orientalists, who began to research Indian language, philosophy, and history. One of these, William Jones, a British judge in Calcutta, fused his extraordinary knowledge of Arabic, Persian, English, Hindi, and Sanskrit to come to the startling theory, now well accepted, that there was a common source of Indian and European languages, now called the Indo-European roots. Jones and others would marvel that Sanskrit, the ancient language of India, was older than English or Latin, and, some would contend, more elegant.

Warren Hastings, a Viceroy of India, founded the Asiatic Society of India in 1784; this society would engage in a study of Indian arts, architecture, and philosophy. Others along the way joined this interest in Indian thought, art, and language, but few became avid students of the Indian healing arts of yoga, Ayurveda, meditation, and the core philosophy of the East—becoming one with creation. Those few who ventured into Indian practices were considered weird, amusing, or downright nutty.

In the swirling activities of British India, there were remarkable Indian men and women, indeed, teachers of extraordinary capabilities. Of course, there were the sham gurus and weird cults, just as there are now in India and America, but there were more than a handful whose names and stories have come down to us, indeed, who are still respected, even revered today in many parts of the globe. We recognize not only spiritual teachers of great wisdom, but also extraordinary musicians, artists, and designers. Even the British, for example, could not help but marvel at the astonishing beauty of Indian temples and mosques.

The Taj Mahal, for example, built by the Muslim architects influenced by Sufism, is recognized as one the most beautiful buildings in the world. But there are countless other examples, as Hindu and Muslim India was thick with monuments, palaces, churches, and temples.

There is a delightful story about one of India's great teachers; the story is very instructive about the British attitude because this man was active during the last years of the Raj. Ramana Maharshi lived in his ashram (teaching center) next to a mountain in Southern India, not far from the great city of Madras. Ramana, who died in 1951, spent most of his life in "British" India, but he lived in his own world, completely untouched by politics or foreign interests.

Ramana, well known in his time, is still respected today. While alive, he was visited by thousands from many countries of our planet. All year, visitors came to his center to witness this man who many consider a saint or holy man, in fact, one of the more notable of the twentieth century. While a Hindu by birth and training, he welcomed people of all faiths as well as those who had no faith. He treated women the same as men, and, indeed, he treated animals with endearing

206

respect. In the end, there is but one God, one creation, and one truth, which no one owns.

His primary goal was to help people wake up to their highest potential, that is, their most essential humanness, which, in truth, is their divinity. He helped others to wake up to a simple and alive awareness, not burdened by egoistic impulses: what the Indians call enlightenment or self-realization. He had no complex teaching or dogma and made no demands. He certainly did not try to persuade people to follow him or his "way." Simplify: That was his teaching. Without going into too many explanations or words, his teaching was based on primary foundations: the study of the great spiritual books of India; the witness of his presence, darshan, which could inspire people to wake up; and the practice of self-observation—to go right down to the core of self. Time and time again, he would ask: What is the source of I-thought? What is the source of ego, or our sense of I, our assumption that we know? Ramana distinguished between the small everyday self and a bigger self that we all can share.

A person might come to visit him—they could be an important businessman or politician, a simple farmer or laborer, or a housewife. They would enter the modest hall where he often sat. They could sit near him. Sometimes he would speak, but often he would not say anything. After some time, the visitor might nod and leave, or stay for some days. This experience was called darshan, often a profound experience for the visitor, one reason so many came to visit, for a day or for weeks. They became peaceful, calm, rejuvenated. They would feel their normal busy "self" drop away for a few hours or longer.

Over the years, many Indians from all over India visited Ramana, and people from many other parts of the globe; but few British Indians. However, his first European student was actually a British Indian policeman, Frank Humphrey, who visited his ashram after an illness. Mr. Humphrey, who worked in the nearby city of Madras, had a dream prior to his first visit where he saw Ramana, an experience that was extraordinary for him since he had never met or seen a picture of the master. Until his retirement, Humphrey worked his job and regularly visited the ashram and when he returned to England, he joined a monastery. He saw no contradiction in this development and, indeed, there was none.

This is an image of Ramana that I found in Arthur Osbourne's book, an excellent examination of this special human being. This copy had notations by my father, who must have made them when living in America.

Arthur Osbourne, an Englishman, was a professor who came to India for one thing: to study with the great teacher whom he had heard about while teaching in Thailand. Paul Bruton, a celebrated writer and philosopher, had visited, asked questions, and was impressed. His subsequent account reached many people and brought Ramana more fame, which he did not seek in any way. He was a quiet, shy, retiring man, but one who, by all accounts, had a very lively presence.

One of the "celebrities" who dropped by was the British writer Somerset Maugham, who in his day was very famous, a writer of best-selling novels. Maugham, like many in the artsy world, had heard rumors of this special Indian holy man, and he visited the ashram one day while on a tour of India. The important writer wanted to check out this guru he had heard so much about. The story is told that Maugham stayed a short time, not more than a few hours, but experienced darshan, which made a deep impression on the celebrated author. He would later write a book about an English seeker traveling to India to meet a special teacher—a study that long preceded the 1960s when Indian practices became the rage. This book, *Razor's Edge*, was later made into a movie with Bill Murray as the lead actor.

Ramana's teaching, a direct product of ancient Indian practice, is alive today. In my father's library I found the Osbourne biography of Ramana Maharshi, purchased in London after Wally had left India. Several passages are marked with pencils. Wally, in his quirky way, became interested in spiritual search early in life—following in the tentative footsteps of his mother—but his search really intensified while he was in Africa. In Rhodesia a Westinghouse loaned him a book called *In Search of the Miraculous*, written by the Russian, Ouspensky, about his encounter with the sage Gurdjieff. From there, Wally traveled to London to meet John Bennet, a British scientist, who pointed him to a man in America.

And in America, Wally went on to study with a distinguished man who taught a practice that, while not "Indian," was related to foundational Indian practices. This man, John Pentland, who had studied with Gurdjieff in Paris, established a center in New York.

Wally and Zizza studied with this man for ten years. Mr. Pentland, a man of great experience and wisdom, would positively influence many Americans. This teaching, by the way, is not a religion or cult; it is a way of living a more aware life, and anyone, of any or no religion, can participate. My mother always spoke highly of John Pentland. He demanded much from his students, but, when he saw they were sincere, he was generous and kind. And in a modest way, Zizza flowered and, in her later years, would manifest a kind and loving presence that many sensed.

EIGHTEEN

THE AMAZING JOURNEY CONTINUES

We return now to the saga of Wally and Zizza. The long ordeal of World War II ended in the spring of 1945. What a glorious spring that was! Around the world people celebrated the end of Nazi aggression. But for many, celebration was accompanied by suffering and confusion. Wally's last war year was spent in the dangerous jungles of Burma, part of the expedition that had paratrooped into the jungle to stem the advance of the Japanese into India. British and American forces slowed that ferocious invasion, but the atom bomb at Hiroshima put an end to Japanese ambitions. Several movies in the 1950s and 1960s, like *Merrill's Marauders*, depict American and British heroics in the Burmese jungles. It was a precarious time, with mistakes made on the Allies' side and many men stranded or wounded in the jungles. My father never mentioned this episode of his life. Not one word. And I would not have known about it had not Zizza mentioned it in her later years when I had asked her what Wally did in the last year of the war.

When the war in Burma ended, the fears in India were erased. Japan would not invade the raj with the astonishing zeal it had displayed in the Far East. Zizza had had five years of worrying about her homeland, under threat from Nazi forces. Kent, where she grew up, had a coastline dotted with fortifications and artillery. But even worse were thoughts about her husband, with only a letter here and there. I can barely imagine what those five years were like for them both.

After the Japanese surrendered, Zizza flew to Calcutta—the nearest Indian city to Burma—to find Wally. The exhausted, sick, and emaciated British soldiers were repatriated to Calcutta. Zizza, hearing that Wally was indeed alive, rushed from hospital to hospital to find him. Some kind captain—she attracted these—helped her locate the tired and worn Wally, recuperating at a British army hospital in the outskirts of the great Asian city. She nursed him back to health, and together they returned to Renala to spend some quiet time with Ysobel and baby Val, the daughter that Wally had barely seen. The resting time, however, was brief. Events in their lives, Renala, India, and the planet, hurtled them forward to a new life elsewhere.

In 1947, when independence came, even those of the British who were prepared were shocked. For many it came fast, right on the heels of the ordeal of World War II. Wally and Zizza, like many of the British, had been making plans to leave for some time. When they left India in the summer of 1947, Renala was alive, even thriving in a modest way. Hazel was in charge, and an old hand she was, capable, knowledgeable, and tough.

For Wally, leaving Renala was a sad and confusing occasion. He and Zizza, like so many other Brits, went to Karachi or Bombay—one of the big ports—and booked a passage onto one of the ships that had plied the waters between India and England for over two centuries. In Bombay, they would stay at the sumptuous colonial hotel, the Taj Mahal, which is still operational.

From 1612, the British had traveled the routes, back and forth, on their way to a new life, a new adventure, or an early death—or back to the green home they had missed for so many years. Wally made that long journey quite a few times. But this time there was no coming back to the land of tropical heat, palm trees, bustling cities, masses of teeming people, and the strange sounds and smells and sights.

How many places in the world can you see a cow wandering the city streets amidst pedestrians and traffic? The cow is a sacred animal. "Ridiculous," the British would murmur as they navigated the narrow, busy streets. How many places can you still see wandering sadhus, holy men, with ash on their simply clad bodies, and bare feet? How many places can you see tremendous rivers, the highest mountains, and the empty horizon of desert? How many places can you see a whole temple carved out of one monstrous rock? Or religious texts that have no date or time? How many places can you see a nine-story entrance to a temple complex covered with thousands of statues of people, gods, and animals? How many places can you see people of all kinds and classes and religions mingling on crowded streets—all with the patina of color, floral decoration, animal aromas, and the multitude of textures. And all different kinds of people: the simple farmers, the wise Brahmins, ambitious bankers, musicians and artists, artisans, factory workers, yogis and swamis, and even ornate Maharajas. Yes, the British often shook their heads, but the lure of Mother India ran deeper than most could admit.

We see Wally, Zizza, and their two young daughters at the banister on the deck as the ship pulls out of the harbor, horns blowing. In the distance, the milling crowds of Hindus; the swaying palms; the sweet aromas; the stench; the cloying heat; the billowing white robes of the Brahmin; and the jewelry and bright sari of the young bride. And gone forever the trumpets, the sounds of the British cavalry in their finest, the parade of Indian and British soldiers, and all the other accessories of an exclusive society that one day dispersed in a flash.

The little girls are excited, running along the deck, bumping into passengers while Zizza, holding her hat, laughing, tries to corral them. Wally turns and smiles, almost yells, then the distant sound, a loud horn; he turns his eyes back to the shore one last time. He looks and looks, as the ship leaves the harbor. He would never return. Two hundred and seventy years ago, the first "Indian" Vanrenen would jump off a ship at the great India port city. Young Jacob, with a simple worn leather knapsack, all he owned, would make his first tentative

An image of street life in India, circa 1980, where life has gone on for hundreds of years: women preparing garlands of flowers for worshippers about to enter the incredible temple in Madras. Where in the West could you find a magical scene like this? I was so enchanted with this scene that I almost forgot to press the button on the camera. The women, polite and charming, did not object to my forward manner. I never thrust my camera around like tourists do, and always kept it hidden. I tried my best to be respectful.

In a desert town in India, far from the big cities, Johnna and I walked around the streets and witnessed a people and world that seemed to be from another century. I snuck this shot with my tiny Minolta of this rugged desert man who wore a dagger in his belt. Unlike me this behavior, but I could not resist this one time. I was glad that he did not see my camera. But, in truth, he was a gentleman, purchasing some sandals from a tiny store. The desert men wear turbans of different colors and brightly decorated slippers and sandals. This chapter of our journey was one of the few times in my life that I have witnessed a place and culture that seemed to be from some fabulous, other world. We were lucky to travel through at that time because I doubt very much it is the same today.

steps on Indian soil, smelling the tropical aromas and watching the colorful parade of Asian life.

It made sense for the time being to return "home" to England; it felt safe and comfortable for Zizza and the little girls. But home was not England for Wally. He was used to big open places; horizons that never ended; and the heat, the sun, and the open sky. He was comfortable in a multicultural society. Back in England, they would make the round of the relatives from both sides of the family, smile at family gatherings, complain about the weather and state of England, and move on. For a short time, Wally tried Ireland. He was restless. He thought of many places, mostly empire vestiges, and even traveled here and there. Ireland was a brief and moderately disastrous fling. England could never work. He had some connections, even roots, in South Africa that in a way was like India: the bright sun, wide open spaces, and opportunity. Next stop: South Africa and Rhodesia.

With Zizza and two young daughters, Wally boarded the steam ship to South Africa, a colony started by the Dutch in the sixteenth century. The Dutch, avid traders, had a port stop in South Africa on their way to lucrative plantations in Asia, but some had emigrated to escape Catholic oppression. Indeed, some of my family came from this Dutch/Germanic root. The English would follow the Dutch and in time create another African colony there. What appealed to Wally and Zizza was that some settled parts of South Africa were quite British, but also resonant of India. Wally's younger brother, Jumbo, had a vineyard in the beautiful hills outside of Cape Town. South Africa was exciting, warm, large, and still filled with opportunity for adventurous Europeans, but Wally wanted something even more adventurous and remote.

He headed north of South Africa to Rhodesia—named after the wealthy colonialist, Cecil Rhodes—a lovely little country in which the British had settled, in search of gold, in about 1900. Gold, while not so plentiful, was surpassed by rich, fertile farm land. Rhodesia was a land of vast plains filled, in those days, with wild animals: lions, giraffes, zebras, and rhinoceros. The white invasion became, in effect, a land grab that pushed the Africans aside. The country became known for its rugged white pioneers, good weather, dramatic African scenery, and abundant farm land. Rhodesia also had a large and bustling African population that had been there for many centuries, and today is called Zimbabwe, after the mysterious tower ruins, now a major tourist attraction.

I am naturally fond of this photograph of Colleta and me, so happy together. In Rhodesia, we lose our star photographers, Ysobel and Louis. My father, not so skilled, is very busy with the tobacco farm, but my mother had an opportunity to pick up a cheap Kodak now and then, and I was always around!

Wally, always different than the crowd (like his wife), bought some farmland, built a little house, and raised his family, which now included Denys, my older brother, and me. For seven years we were Rhodesians, living on the edge of nowhere in the bright African sun and under a clear blue sky. Today what I remember best were the Africans who were such a big part of life on the farm. I remember them well, their faces and jobs: there was Johnny, my friend; Sinoa, the cook; and Robert, the truck driver. They were the first smiling faces, besides my parents and siblings, of my living mythology, the forces that would imprint in my essence and memory.

Val, looking tall and lovely, Johnny, and little me. Even though Johnny was quite a bit older than I, we were friends. I remember well the games we used to engage in, and my trips to the African compound where he offered me a local delicacy: fried flying ants. Perhaps he became a freedom fighter for his people when Rhodesia became embroiled in a civil war in the 1970s. A black African nation would emerge, proudly called Zimbabwe, after the mysterious and evocative ruins, now a major tourist attraction. Today, most people who visit Zimbabwe will travel to the Zimbabwe ruins, rock towers and walls, and Victoria Falls, one of the spectacular waterfalls of the planet, but also a place where one can stay in a lodge and witness elephants, lions, and giraffe.

In this photo Caroline and I sit with Ricky, our little terrier. I was lucky to have two older sisters, but they were quite a bit older than me. I played with my African friend, Johnny, or my brother, but obviously I loved the little dog, as my last memory of Rhodesia was Ricky. He ran after the car as we left for the station to catch the train south through the Kalahari Desert to South Africa, and the port in Cape Town. It is my first memory of the sadness of parting.

As in India, the British had built extensive railroad lines to benefit travel and trade. About this trip to South Africa, I have a dim memory of a stop where the train watered. Bushmen, tribal desert people and not black African, were selling trinkets through the windows. I think I—well, my mother—purchased a little bow and arrow. Years later, I would read Lawrence Van der Posts account of his time with the dwindling Bushmen, a people from a timeless world, and living at one with each other and nature. In the modern age they have been treated poorly by Black and White Africans.

Two Rhodesian farm boys, my brother, Denys, to the right. I think I lost the last tussle! Below, my mother and I.

In Rhodesia, I was not opposed to cavorting in the mud without any clothes on. My few years in Rhodesia were marked by my first impressions of life, and what dramatic experiences there were! Lions in the distance, the presence of alligators in the lakes, the warning for poisonous snakes, and the often-exuberant African population.

I also put my mother to fright several times: one time I had emergency surgery to remove a piece of wood that I had inadvertently swallowed. Playing outside, I picked up a tiny piece of wood and put it in my mouth. It went down my throat and got stuck. My mother heard my cry and came running out of the house. I was too young to speak, even if I could, and no one knew why I was breathing so hard. Fortunately, there was a clinic not too far away with a capable doctor who saved my life. Years later Zizza told me that the doctor, named Playfair, was out golfing at seven in the morning when the call came out to attend to me. He rushed in, examined me, and said: if I don't cut his throat open, this little boy will die.

In the next photo I am very pleased, having used up one of my nine lives! I am decently dressed, almost as if I was going to school, but in Rhodesia I was too young for school; my brother and sisters went to schools. These schools were only for the children of European descent. Rhodesia, in those days, had a tight, small European community of mostly farmers, often rugged pioneers from England and other countries. Those who settled there were independent, adventurous people escaping from the tedium of middle class life. Some were escaping

from political or personal crises. It was a hard life for many, but filled with incredible impressions, especially for those living in the "outback" with the lions and giraffe. Rhodesia is a beautiful country with rivers, plains, farms and hills, and blessed with sunny weather and blue sky.

Most of us occasionally wonder about our early years. Before four, I think few of us have memories, but starting about four we can remember vivid experiences: these might provide a glimpse into what kind of person would soon emerge. I had several of these formative experiences in Rhodesia, one I would like to describe.

One day we visited a remote farm for a birthday of a lad around my age. There was a small gathering outside the house, a Rhodesian barbeque. Another boy and I naughtily wandered out back and into the wild bush. We did not go far, but far enough to come upon a giant rock, perhaps eight feet high. We stared at it in wonder: it was covered with ancient bush men rock paintings.

Their rock art is some of the most beautiful in the world, and this rock displayed world class paintings, delicate and finely depicted images of people and animals in motion. Hearing our names being called, we turned and rushed back to civilization. It is my first encounter (or memory) with native art, and my first memory of the sense of wonder. In our culture we do not value the sense of wonder enough—we are too busy and too head centered. A respected German thinker once said that the sense of wonder is a most precious feeling. Without wonder, and all the feelings it gives birth to, we would have less art, poetry, stories, and authentic religion.

Louis with three admirers

Wally and Zizza lived in Africa for almost a decade. What a decade that was, with many chapters and adventures! But Wally, who had good insight, saw that Africa was best for the Africans, and that the "white" era was ending. He decided to move on. Where to now? The empire was imploding. Well, let's try the old country again. That seemed logical! Off the young family went to England, taking the United Castle line from Cape Town to Southampton, England. The voyage of thousands of miles was a marvel for a little boy.

England, however, did not suit Wally's restless soul: it was still cold, damp, small, no bright Indian sun; worse, England was socialist—heaven forbid. I don't know where he got the idea of moving to America, an original colony, but that he did—and it was a brilliant decision. No other immediate relatives had moved to America—there was no precedent in our family. I suspect that high English taxes and American opportunity attracted the insightful Wally. But there was another attraction.

In England he met a British man, John Bennet. He said to Wally, if you go to America, I have a man you should meet. This man, John

Pentland, is a highly respected teacher. There Wally would learn meditation and self-observation in his inner journey, subjects only just coming into attention twenty years later.

Ironic that he would be learning practices and ideas that had existed in India for generations. But the British in India were notoriously blind to the powerful undercurrent of spiritual life in India, a life that was about as varied as one of those amazing Indian temples covered with stone sculpture. But at the core of Indian spirituality, as ancient as time, was a contemplative core that was truly enlivening. At least once a day one has to, for a short time, become silent and attentive, and in this way find the pulse of life that we all share.

So today in America one can study meditation, spiritual reflection, and yoga in every state of the Union. In the *Harvard Medical School Newsletter*, which I receive, they include positive articles about meditation, tai chi, and yoga. Let us surmise that in a subconscious way, Wally was influenced by the ambience of Mother India. And like his mother, he had a reflective side, and following the disaster of World War II and his many changes, he turned to a deep search for guidance and meaning in life.

In 1957, the family boarded the famous ocean liner Queen Elizabeth, and landed at the Cunard docks around 42nd Street in Manhattan. Wally considered dairy farming in upstate New York, but another unusual situation opened up. Wally and family settled in a scenic but modest house between two lakes in a place called Tuxedo Park, about an hour by car from New York City. He would devote some of his time to the stock market and make occasional trips to Wall Street. And both Zizza and Wally regularly went into Manhattan to meet their teacher, John Pentland.

Wally and Zizza's amazing journey includes their life in New York State, not far from Manhattan, and their last and wonderful years in Boulder, Colorado. I know one reason why Wally decided on this big Western state, and in those days not so fashionable. It was a little like India: It had some indigenous people (Chicanos and Indians); it was big, with lots of space, and the sun shone 320 days of the year; and it had glorious scenic mountains, a major feature in the part of India that Wally had lived in. Once again, he made a brilliant decision: he chose a marvelous destination.

Wally, in his prime, on a very happy day. This was a younger Wally, pre-World War II, prior to the departure from Renala and the tragic death of his mother.

Zizza—in her prime— not long after the wedding and her modve to India, with the immortal Gaffy Waffy, their beloved dachshund. She is about the same age as Wally in the above photo. This photo was taken by Wally in 1939 at a playing field in Lahore. You can see the cricket players in the background. The terrible war started soon after the photograph was taken, and Wally would be called to fight overseas. He and his Central India Horse (with no horses), including Indian officers and soldiers, would travel to a most inhospitable world, North Africa, to tackle Rommel and his mighty Nazi army.

A delightful image of Wally, the former British cavalryman, holding his granddaughter Natasha, my sister Caroline's child. He is nearing the end of his long, full life, and one can say that he had mellowed some. It is interesting how photographs can surprise and reveal hidden facts. He is at ease and relaxed, and, strangely enough, he looks a little like an Indian gentleman. There were times in his later years when he, Zizza, and I would share an afternoon tea in the afternoon in the shade of a willow tree. We never abandoned the English tradition of teatime, and these peaceful interludes were cherished by all.

A proud Wally looks on as Johnna and I sign our wedding papers on the celebration day. Johnna, always practical, is showing me where to sign! We knew that the wedding would act as a smokescreen for our respective parents, because in a few days we would fly to India for our extended honeymoon—over six months! We had planned and saved for over a year, and we were determined to do a once-in-a lifetime adventure. But before we left, we did not want any grumbling from them!

225

At the wedding the meeting of Wally and Johnna's father, John, an Italian American, provided some laughs after John, a gregarious man, came up to Wally and vigorously shook his hand. "Well, Walter, congratulations," he said. "I am about to gain a son, and you a daughter!" Wally peered at this stranger, paused (they had barely met and Wally was a little absent-minded) and responded: "And who are you?" John never tired of telling this story.

When we returned from Asia, we would encounter a new life in Boulder, jobs and responsibilities, and in a few months the sudden death of Wally at the relatively young age of 69. In this photo—I just noticed—Wally is wearing his Clifton College tie, a memento of his school days in England.

Many people, once they reach their late sixties and seventies, have lived an amazing life with many vivid chapters in diverse places. Wally's life had followed the dramatic trajectory of the twentieth century: from Edwardian England to British India, then Africa and post-war England and Ireland, and then two great locations in America. He rode in the cavalry when it was more than a show, had fought the Nazis in World War II, and suffered in the Asian conflict against Japan. In a grand climax, he enjoyed over two decades in the ebullient America of the 1960s and 1970s, experiencing, even, the wild sixties with rock music, hippies, and war demonstrations. He struggled to keep his sons out of the Vietnam War. Neither of us went to that war. Though a conservative in politics, he detested that war, and any war, and in the end became a spiritual seeker practicing ancient practices from Asia. And his faithful—and patient—wife would follow a similar path, exceeding Wally's history by 30 years.

She was living now in Boulder, Colorado in America, her fourth continent. A former Edwardian girl in Kent, wife to British Indian cavalry officer, pioneer in Africa, and, finally, settling down in trendy Boulder, Colorado, five minutes from the great Rocky Mountains. She would become spiritual midwife to many.

Zizza's last 30 years, until she was 92, were good, as she had settled into her Boulder lifestyle with friends, spiritual companions, part-time work, and, of course, treks into the mountains. I, living near

226

Zizza in her seventies on an outing into the mountains of Colorado in September when the aspens are turning yellow. She loved these jaunts into the mountains, so very different from Kent, England where she was raised, but reminiscent of the mountains of Northern India.

Boston, would visit her whenever I could. We always enjoyed each other's company and treasured our little rituals: afternoon teatime with a cup of warm Tetley's, jaunts into the mountains, lunch with friends at the Tibetan restaurant downtown, chats with Rod or Viv, and endless discussions about this and that. We shared a deep interest in spiritual matters, in nature, and in living with gusto. Around ninety she really began to age and took a downturn in her overall health.

One morning in early September, 2010, I got a call from Boulder. At the advice of her alert nurse, I rushed to the airport, flew from Boston to Denver, and traveled by car to Boulder as fast as I could. Into the nursing home I ran, anxious to see her. She was weak, very weak, and barely coherent, but still able to travel in a wheelchair. Little did I know it, but when I took her out into the sun and flowers, it would be our last outing. Over 59 years I had taken thousands of outings with her as we loved our excursions into nature. Way back in Rhodesia, we had ventured into the gardens together, I a toddler and she a vibrant brunette. On this last walk, I was blissfully naïve about a quick and dramatic end. It seemed impossible that she would die. She was frail and did not speak as I wheeled her outside. As so often in the past, we admired the day, the gardens, and we were quite alone, then as the sun settled down over the Rockies, shadows and cool descended onto the garden. I took her inside for a well-needed rest. She said a few words, but their meaning escaped me. Her old friend Libby came by so I, feeling exhausted from a very long day, went to my room for the night.

That night I was staying with Vicki, my niece, at her condo, and in the early morning I woke from an exhausted sleep with a start. I jumped from bed, dressed quickly, and rushed to the nursing home. I was alone with her in her room when she died mid-morning, September 10, 2010. At the last moment, an old friend, Marshall, stopped by on his way to work, not knowing that Zizza was passing. It was not a coincidence, and I was glad to have a reliable companion. It was an honor for the two of us to be there in her final moments. And it was then that I began to understand how important it is to accompany someone on this final journey.

She had lived a good life into the twenty-first century and had seen so much in social and historical change. Her marriage, an adventure for sure and not all "roses," occupied almost 40 years of her life. She had first met a handsome Wally when a young lady of 19, a child of a little village in the backroads of Kent. And, like Wally, she died on a sunny warm day with a view of the blue sky and the mountains. I present as the last image, a flawed photograph from Uncle Louis' collection, an enduring image of the end and the beginning of the journey.

EPILOGUE

In ancient Greek, "epilogue" means "after the book." Wally and Zizza's life on this planet has ended, but their legacy and influence live on. Our family is not the only one to have many exciting chapters. Every family has a unique and interesting history, a journey through time and into the future, and bound by many commonalities: a love for each other, a sharing of all the dramas of life from birth to marriage, childbirth to burial, as well as loss and happiness—and, of course, disappointments. I well know how many so-called dysfunctional families there are. But we all come from one source, whatever you want to call it, from which all families have emerged over a vast amount of time.

The triumph of Wally and Zizza can be seen in their offspring, so vital and varied. My brother Denys and his wife Ellen have three grown children, all who have children—a handsome group of people.

Our American branch of the Vanrenen "clan," the offspring of Wally and Zizza—which now is more than thirty people—can thank the efforts of Wally and Zizza for their lives in America. We can be proud to say that we have become a multi-national clan with varied influences: French-Canadian (Lorraine), Cajun (Viv and Rod), Italian, Indian (!), Chinese, and even Hawaiian (Bessie's wonderful husband, Jared, has a Hawaiian and German background). Denys, my brother, married Ellen Mignone, whose family came from Italy, and like so

Denys and Ellen with their growing family. Ellen, so happy with all her grandchildren, is laughing.

many Americans created a new life in New Jersey. Denys, however, would meet Ellen while traveling in Europe as a young roustabout.

We owe much to Ysobel and Denys Henry, who founded Renala, a major investment of time and energy. And we should not forget the people of India. We are all children of the amazing journey of Wally and Zizza. And those reading who are not of this family can relate as they, too, are part of an amazing journey that reaches back generations, and forward into the unknown. We all share a similar background and many key life experiences, in particular our deep wish for acceptance and love.

Families grow and change, and are often the intersection of completely different tributaries, which makes for diversity and interest. I met Lorraine and we introduced to each other completely

Lorraine with Lucky, our lovely cat, who we enjoyed for twenty years. Lorraine and I share a love for animals and nature and have spent many days hiking and exploring New England, Colorado, and elsewhere. Lorraine has a diverse background with many interests, particularly ecology, nature, and plants. The old farming instinct, which we share, is given an outlet in our various gardens. We have created a very modest Renala garden with the same passion as Ysobel, my grandmother.

The photograph below is Lorraine and her mother, Eva Rubinacci, whose life history has intrigued me. For one, Eva worked in the last, giant textile mills in New England. With a French-Canadian background, Eva still speaks French, and at every major holiday we celebrate at her bounteous table.

different families and backgrounds. This is true of so many friends and families I know, and it is a source of creativity and discovery in life. It can also be a source of friction, but as long as there is love and respect, friction can result in new understanding. Without new ideas and influences, families can stagnate, not thrive and grow, and the new will wilt like a tree in early frost.

Wally and Zizza's journey lives on. There were hard years, happiness, great suffering and losses, several wars, four continents, and many varied experiences. They lived a good life in their last years and arrived at a place of inner peace, despite aging and continual challenges. And they were fortunate that Wally had chosen America, a relatively healthy country with opportunity and justice.

Wally, never rich, could not have afforded to move to America without the financial backing of the money he had received from his portion of Renala with its fabulous race horses. In a sense the story of Renala is still alive. With this backing, he was able to start a new life in America; afford a comfortable home; and send his children to college. Caroline, my darling sister, died in 1994, but she left three wonderful children, Anita, Natasha, and Dylan, all living in various Eastern states.

Anita, with the red shirt (Cal's second child), and Karen on a mountain hike. Anita, in the tradition of our roaming family, was born in New Zealand, and she and Karen now live in Charleston, South Carolina. Our family is reaching into many distant and familiar places! Anita and Karen share a zest for life, and Anita, from my perspective, has an unforgettable laugh.

Natasha and her family: Jonathan, Natasha, Chloe, Richard, and Aron. Natasha was born in England, and I remember her from a little baby; now a mature and lovely lady with grown children. She now lives outside of Philadelphia in New Jersey. In jest I call her the "Jersey" girl of the family, and she responds with that happy laugh that is one of her trademarks.

Val's children, Vivienne and Roderick, live in Colorado and owe much to their beloved grandmother, Zizza, who raised them after Val's premature death.

Below is a photograph of a young Roderick and Simba on a mountain in Colorado. For several months, while his mother was ill, I looked after Rod and took him on numerous little adventures with Simba our beloved golden retriever. Incredibly, forty-eight years have transpired since I took this photograph.

The photograph below is of Bessie and Jared in a silly mood with their delightful children. Bessie, Denys' daughter, lives in Denver with Jared, Maurice, and Sebastian. Both are natural parents; they are a lucky group; and both parents are gifted writers.

This photo shows happy Vivienne, sister Val's daughter, with her daughter Lorelai. Vivienne has lived in Denver for many years, and now Vanrenens live in Central, Western and Eastern America. The extended family prospers in Australia, South Africa, England, America, and many other places. Until recently, I had no idea how many Vanrenens there are on this planet! One branch has even started a Facebook site!

Dylan Horsely, sister Cal's son, with his wife, Liz, and children, Alexander and Asherah.
Dylan, born in America, lives in Pennsylvania with his charming little family.

My children born of Johnna Albi, whose family are Italian and Irish—we are covering all the bases here—are prospering in San Francisco. Tragically for us all, Johnna died in 1995. Currently, I live in Massachusetts with Lorraine Rubinacci, whose family is from Italy, England, and French Canada. Her family has had a fascinating saga, and Lorraine, a product of many cultural influences, bears the charm of her varied genetic background. I am happy to be a good friend of her (still) vivacious mother, Eva.

My son, Gabriel, married Maria Ly, whose parents escaped from Vietnam after the war. Generously, Canada welcomed them and for some years they struggled to create a prosperous life on a new continent. Nu and Mindy were blessed with two lovely daughters, Maria and Kim, both of whom are exceptionally intelligent and considerate. Maria, whose roots are Chinese, is my daughter-in-law, a fact that is most pleasing. Ariana, my daughter, recently married Sameer Pangrekar, whose parents came from India! Abhay and Chitra emigrated to America—just like the Vanrenens—for education and opportunity, and this is where Sameer was born and raised. Zizza is probably clapping her hands with glee. We are so happy to have Sameer in our family. He, by the way, is pure Californian, and a great fan of golf and football. Here are some of their wedding shots at a vineyard in California.

Epilogue

At their wonderful "vineyard" wedding, Ariana and Sameer would perform an Indian dance for which they had secretly trained. To the great surprise of the wedding party, about 150 people, they came out into the hall in Indian finery from toe to head—stunning outfits, traditional dance dress. And the Indian music started. Everyone sat up. Ariana and Sameer enchanted us all with a perfectly executed Indian wedding dance and not a five-minute exercise!

On April 10—my brother's birthday—2017, Maria, Gabe's wife, gave birth to their first child, a boy called Lorenzo. In typical Maria fashion, she arrived in the San Francisco hospital in labor, and delivered the baby in five minutes. So now Wally and Zizza have several great-grandchildren, which they would be very happy for. They have an Indian son-in-law and a little baby who is part Chinese descent. Below we see pictures of Maria and Gabriel with their son, Lorenzo, and finally Lorenzo by himself, a fresh little baby, and the most recent grandchild to flag the journey of Wally and Zizza. Lorenzo, and his numerous cousins, represent the tip of the new branch, the chain of family growing into the future and reaching way back in time. We, the human family, are all connected.

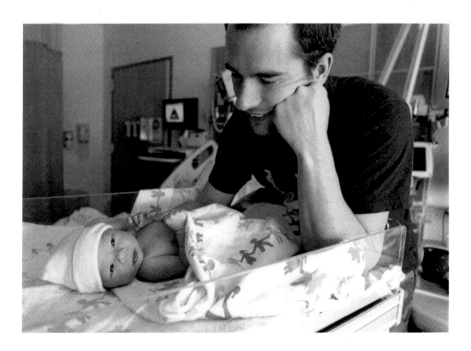

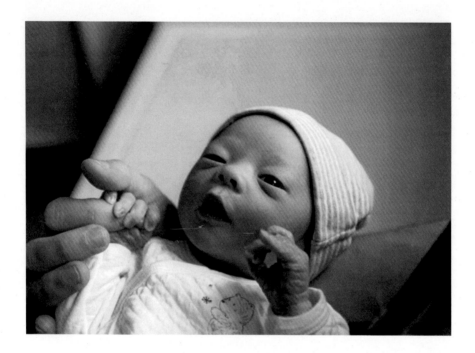

ABOUT THE AUTHOR

Louis Vanrenen has experienced a long and wonderful journey in his life: from Southern Africa to England by old fashioned ocean liner, then across the Atlantic to America where he has spent good time in New York, Colorado, and Massachusetts. For much of this time he was blessed with the company of his parents. Currently, he lives south of Boston with his partner, Lorraine, and cat, Sunshine. They enjoy their restored historical home, and maintain gardens of flowers, trees, and vegetables. Louis also enjoys visiting Gabriel and Ariana, his two children, in San Francisco, where he sees Maria and Sameer, and his grandson, Lorenzo.

He has written several books, taught and lectured about health, and operates an acupuncture clinic where he focuses on chronic pain and wellness. A pioneer in his field, he has studied and taught Asian healing practices, including yoga, nutrition, chi kung and meditation. From an early age, Louis has kept a journal, now fifty years in the making, and he is also a writer of poetry: "Something that came naturally to me from an early age." He practices meditation and has engaged in a lifelong pursuit of happiness and health, helped by the example of his parents and teachers.